BELONGING TO GOD
Catechism Resources for Worship

GENEVA

Geneva Press
Louisville, Kentucky

Book design by Sharon Adams
Cover design by Pam Poll Graphic Design
Cover illustration: Gertrud Mueller Nelson

First edition
Published by Geneva Press
Louisville, Kentucky

This book is printed on acid-free paper that meets the American National Standards Institute Z39.48 standard. ∞

PRINTED IN THE UNITED STATES OF AMERICA

03 04 05 06 07 08 09 10 11 12 — 10 9 8 7 6 5 4 3 2 1

Library of Congress Cataloging-in-Publication Data

Belonging to God : catechism resources for worship.— 1st ed.
    p. cm.
ISBN 0-664-50236-9 (alk. paper)
    1. Presbyterian Church—Catechisms. I. Geneva Press.

BX9184 .B45 2003
238'5137—dc21

                                                              2002028605

Contents

Foreword

*T*he generations of those who memorized the Westminster Shorter Catechism as an expected ritual of growing up are almost gone. A vast majority of the "young old" and all who were born after them have had little or no exposure to the succinct and direct biblical and theological understandings of being Presbyterian Christians. For many of them, education in the church, if people availed themselves of it, was quite often narrative, episodic, or solely an experience of learning Bible content. So, what have they missed? A language, a framework of convictions, a historic compendium of the beliefs on which the church and its ordered life are based.

For our ancestors in faith, the Catechism was often a Sunday afternoon discipline of memorizing words. Some of the words would be heard again in the liturgy of worship. Many of the words, once satisfactorily memorized, would surface only when a relative or minister put out a question to test the retention of what had been learned. For many this was not a happy memory.

Responding to several realities in the church in the waning years of the last century, and perhaps also to the prompting of the Holy Spirit, our church "redid" the Catechism so that its language would seem more familiar to us today. In a further effort, a catechism for children was created.

One has only to listen to children in school or at play to realize that they both know and use the language of the day, even of the moment. They pick it up quickly and redo it as the "in" and "out" phrases of our culture are born and quickly become obsolete. Children hear the culture's language in the media, often at home, on the playground, in their sports, music, and other pastimes.

Our faith also has a language. Unlike the culture, however, our faith language points to and makes verbal, enduring truths and values. It is a foundation and a framework. It is a foundation on which we are built into the body of Christ, a body with a head who is Jesus Christ; we are given guidance for living as God's people and Christ's ministers in the world God made, loves, and redeems. It is a framework against which we measure our human aspirations, practices, and possibilities.

Children learn through experience in multiple settings. When home, school, and neighborhood embody, and thus teach, the same values with similar languages, children are quick to take them for their own. So it is in the church. To hear, see, and experience language in classroom, worship, choir, and fellowship groups is to hasten incorporation and understanding. Because many adults are returning to church after lengthy absences or are coming for the first time, the same holds true for them. Repetition brings familiarity and a sense of belonging. The language and the truths expressed by it make it easier to claim our faith and to ask questions that can lead to deeper understanding and commitment.

At some level we all like to "know," to be on the inside of what is going on and not left to be an observer. Children feel empowered when they can do what adults do and begin to understand what adults say. Repetition often brings curiosity that pushes one into further knowing. Hearing words and phrases in the music, prayers, and liturgy of worship teaches more than just the intellect. The worship service—replete with acts and symbols, with various levels and kinds of participation, with the mystery that surrounds the God we can't see and God's people who stand and sit and speak with us—becomes a powerful context for learning. The language of the Catechism, our way of saying who we are and who we know God to be, belongs to our children as well as to adults. So does the worship life of the church. Incorporating the Catechism into the worship service invites learning that is not mere memorization but a participation and a place within the community—a place and a way of saying why we are there and who it is that we gather to worship. This liturgical resource is a rich gift to pastors, educators, and parents, but most importantly it's a gift to our children.

Freda A. Gardner
Moderator,
211th General Assembly (1999)

Acknowledgments

We gratefully acknowledge the generous gift from the First Presbyterian Church of Dallas Foundation, which enabled us to commission the original art, hymn text, and Lord's Prayer setting. The Office of Theology and Worship and Geneva Press provided additional funds.

The writing team was called together by the Office of Theology and Worship and included the Rev. Dr. Martha Moore-Keish, Associate for Worship; the Rev. Dr. Rob Carlson, Pastor of The Presbyterian Church, Okemos, Michigan; the Rev. Rebecca Davis, Children's Defense Fund; Martha Bess DeWitt, Director of Christian Education, Westminster Presbyterian Church, Nashville, Tennessee; and the Rev. Dr. Fane Downs, Buffalo Gap, Texas. Mary Jane Cooper developed the list of musical resources keyed to the major themes of the catechism.

We appreciate the editorial help of David Dobson of the Geneva Press for bringing this collection to publication.

Introduction

Belonging to God: Catechism Resources for Worship is designed to bring the language, thus the teaching of the church (the catechesis), into the worship of God's people. Three catechisms were approved for study by the 210th General Assembly (1998) of the PC(USA): *Belonging to God: A First Catechism; The Study Catechism: Confirmation Version;* and *The Study Catechism: Full Version.* The 210th General Assembly (1998) instructed the General Assembly Council, through its Office of Theology and Worship, to develop ways of using *Belonging to God: A First Catechism* as a means of involving children in congregational worship and to explore various possibilities of preaching the catechisms. This resource is part of that effort.

Catechisms are intended primarily as instruction; this instruction takes place in formal and informal ways—including in worship. Catechisms encourage conversation among the faithful (not simply rote memorization); their language carries the collective wisdom of the church about our foundational beliefs. They are one way that the faith is handed on from one generation to the next. Catechisms have long been used to prepare the "uninitiated." Young baptized members come to understand and confess the faith for themselves; older ones reinforce their faith commitments. As the language makes its home in hearts and minds, the theology that is expressed makes its home there as well.

In worship the community of faith is formed as God's own people, the priesthood of all believers. Using the language of the catechisms in worship makes explicit the faith commitments of the church. The language of the First Catechism is simple and straightforward, lending itself well to some portions of the church's liturgy. The more complex formulations of the Study Catechisms may be used as well. Because liturgy is "the work of the people," it is appropriate that the language of the catechisms joins the language of Scripture and church tradition in the worship of the people.

This resource is not intended as an end in itself; rather, the authors hope that worship leaders will see how the catechisms can be adapted for worship and will compose their own texts for worship using these models as guides. We hope also that this resource will draw the church into conversation with the new catechisms and with the historic confessional documents in the *Book of Confessions.*

Soli Deo Gloria!

How to Use This Resource

Belonging to God is organized in a manner similar to the *Book of Common Worship*. Chapter 1 includes elements of the Service for the Lord's Day: calls to worship, prayers of the day, calls to confession, prayers of confession, declarations of forgiveness, prayers of illumination, affirmations of faith, other affirmations, the sacraments of Baptism and Eucharist, prayers of the people, and charges and blessings.

Chapter 2 focuses on Proclamation; it includes themes for preaching the catechisms and several stories that may be incorporated into sermons or used independently. Chapter 3 provides Resources for the Liturgical Year, Chapter 4 suggests ways to use the catechism on Special Occasions, and chapter 5 describes uses of the catechism in Alternative Worship settings. Chapter 6 lists Book and Music Resources. Two new musical resources commissioned for this book are included: a hymn text (Mary Jackson Cathey) and a setting of the Lord's Prayer suitable for children or congregational singing (John Horman). Original art by Gertrud Mueller Nelson throughout the book may be reproduced for bulletins and other church publications.

Citations indicate the catechism and question number. Accompanying several of the liturgies are suggestions for their use or suggestions for alternative forms.

Abbreviations

BCW	*Book of Common Worship*
BC	*Book of Confessions*
FC	*Belonging to God: A First Catechism*
SC: CV	*Study Catechism: Confirmation Version*
SC	*Study Catechism*
PH	*Presbyterian Hymnal*

Chapter 1

Service for the Lord's Day
Order with Liturgical Texts

CALLS TO WORSHIP

1

Who are you?

I am a child of God.

Who are we?

We are children of God, the family of faith.

What does it mean to be children of God?

**We belong to God who loves us and calls us God's own.
In life and death we belong to God.**

*Worship leader may pour water into the baptismal font and say,
"Children of God, welcome home."*

Let us worship God together. (FC 1–2)

2

What is this company?

This is the company of the children of God, gathered in God's holy name.
(FC 1)

Where do you come from?

We come from all places, that we may become brothers and sisters in one place. (SC 66)

What is your purpose?

To worship God, to love one another, and to respect all that God has created. (FC 6)

3

The grace of the Lord Jesus Christ, the love of God, and the communion of the Holy Spirit be with all of you. (SC 1)

And also with you.

Let us give thanks this day for God's wonderful goodness. *(SC 2)*

God's steadfast love endures forever.

Because God first loved us, (SC 3)

let us love one another.

Gathered in this community of faith, God invites us to grow in grace and knowledge;

we would offer praise and thanksgiving and good works for the glory of God. (SC 4)

4

Like a shepherd searches for a lost lamb, (FC 25)

so God seeks and saves the lost.

In Christ, God feeds, heals, blesses, and befriends God's people. (FC 26)

Christ has taught us not to fear, but to trust in God always.

By sending Jesus, God welcomes all (FC 13)

into a new life of hope and blessing.

5

Who is this God whom we have come to worship?

God is the Creator of all.

The creator of birds and trees, wind and sea?

God is the Creator of all things seen and unseen.

Then let us worship the God of creation,
the God of all things great and small. (FC 7)

6

In the beginning God created all that is, seen and unseen.

Created in God's own image, we reflect God's goodness, wisdom, and love. (FC 7, 9)

We are the people who believe the good news about Jesus.

By our worship may the Spirit renew us so we may serve God in love. (FC 35)

7

Our help is in the name of the Lord who made heaven and earth.

What did God do to help us?

God chose the people of Israel to make a new beginning.

They received God's covenant and prepared the way for Jesus to come as our Savior.

Let us worship the God of the covenant, the God of heaven and earth. (FC 14)

8

God called Abraham and Sarah.

God calls us.

God blessed the peoples of the earth through God's covenant with Abraham and Sarah.

God uses us to be a blessing in the world and a sign of God's everlasting covenant.

Let us worship and serve God this day and every day. (FC 15–16)

9

When Moses gathered the people of Israel, God said,

"I am the Lord your God
who brought you out of the land of Egypt,
out of the house of slavery."

As we gather here today,
let us worship the Lord,
who continues to be our God
and who still brings us out of the places of our bondage. (FC 18)

10

We are God's people set on a journey of faith together.
How shall we live life together on this journey?

We shall live according to God's commandments given to our forebears
in the wilderness.

What is the main point of these commandments?

We shall love the Lord our God with all our heart, mind, and strength;
and we shall love our neighbor as ourselves.

Then let us worship the Lord together. (FC 18–19)

11

The Spirit gathers us to worship God
and builds us up in faith, hope, and love,
so that we may go into the world to proclaim the gospel
and work for justice and peace. (FC 38)
Let us worship God together.

PRAYERS OF THE DAY

1

Almighty God,
Your love for us and for all people is powerful beyond measure.
Your love is so vast that nothing will prevail against it.
We know this love is trustworthy because of Jesus Christ:
his life of compassion, death on the cross, and resurrection from the dead.
In life and death we belong to you, Holy Triune God,
Father, Son, and Holy Spirit. **Amen**. (SC 7–9)

2

Creator God,
You made all that is, both seen and unseen.
You made us in your image, both male and female,
that we might reflect your goodness, wisdom, and love.
As we gather around Word and Table this day,
may our faith be renewed that we may serve you. **Amen.**
(FC 7–9, 45)

3

God our Father,
We call on you like little children because we know
that you love us and care for us like a loving parent.
Because your Son Jesus prayed to you as Father,
so we pray this way.
You created us to live with you and ask for your help and guidance.
Amen. (FC 46, 50)

CALLS TO CONFESSION

1

What is special about human beings?

God made us, male and female, in the image of God.

What does it mean that we are made in God's image?

It means we are made to reflect God's goodness, wisdom, and love.

Why then do we often act in destructive and hateful ways?

Because we have turned away from God and fallen into sin. (FC 8–10)

2

In spite of God's love for us and gift of love to us,
we often act in destructive and hateful ways.
We close our hearts to God and disobey God's law. (FC 2–3, 10–11)
Together let us confess our sin.

3

Why do we need to confess our sins?

By telling God we are sorry, we ask God not to hold our sins against us, but to accept us again by grace. (FC 56)

Let us confess our sins before God and one another.

Or

A child asks, What do we mean when we pray, "Forgive us our sins"? (FC 56)

Then proceed with congregational response above.

4

(May be used with Prayer of Confession #5 below.)

God gave the people a covenant as an everlasting agreement and vowed to love us and be our hope forever; we vowed to worship and serve only God.

Did the people of God keep covenant with God?

Though some remained faithful, the people too often showed us how much we all disobey God's law. Let us confess our unfaithfulness . . . (FC 15, 16, 20)

5

To say that we have kept covenant with God is to deceive ourselves. But God who always keeps covenant is waiting to bring us back into faithfulness. Let us confess our sins before God and one another. (FC 20–21)

6

(May be used with Prayer of Confession #7 below. The reading of the commandments may also come after the declaration of forgiveness, as God's good gift of the law to guide our living.)

The people of God gathered to hear God's law. God spoke to Moses and said,

"I am the Lord your God who brought you out of the land of Egypt, out of the house of slavery:

  (1) You shall have no other gods before me.
  (2) You shall not make for yourself an idol.
  (3) You shall not make wrongful use of the name of the Lord your God.
  (4) Remember the Sabbath day and keep it holy.
  (5) Honor your father and your mother.
  (6) You shall not murder.
  (7) You shall not commit adultery.
  (8) You shall not steal.
  (9) You shall not bear false witness against your neighbor.
 (10) You shall not covet what is your neighbor's." (FC 18)

Let us confess before God and one another that we do not always live according to God's law.

7

(This summary of the law may also be used following the declaration of forgiveness.)

The Lord gave to Moses the Ten Commandments to instruct us on how to live.

What is the main point of these commandments?

You shall love the Lord your God with all your heart, mind, and strength; and you shall love your neighbor as yourself. Let us confess that we have failed to keep these commandments. (FC 19)

PRAYERS OF CONFESSION

1

Merciful God,
We are like willful children who have turned from you.
We have closed our hearts to you and disobeyed your law.
We do not love you with our whole hearts.
We do not love our neighbors as much as we love ourselves.
Forgive us.
Help us to turn back to you and receive forgiveness. (FC 11, 19)

2

Merciful God,
We give you thanks, for you have created us to live together in love and
    freedom with you, with one another, and with the world.
You have made us in your image
and endowed us with gifts of reason, imagination, and will.
We have been created in order that your goodness might be reflected in
    our lives, but we have fallen short of your glory. (SC 16)

Our relations with others are distorted and confused. (FC 12)
Though we live with neighbors, we have ceased to live for them.
Though we live with you, we have ceased to live for you.
Although we recognize our distinctive human gifts,
we have not used those gifts well.
Our hearts have been set on self—not others,
and certainly not on you, O God. (SC 16, 20)
Lord, have mercy upon us.

3

Eternal God,
We confess that we have too often acted as if we can earn your love
and have forgotten your free gift of grace.
We want to impress you and others,
but we have lost our way.
Forgive us when we forget that we are your children
and find our identity in the messages of our culture
rather than your Word.
Help us to live as your heirs, children who belong to you,
who love us more than we can understand.
Show us how to love and trust you with all our hearts.
In Christ our brother and our Lord.
(FC 1–3, 5)

4

Merciful God,
We confess that we close our hearts to you.

You hate our sin but never stop loving us.

We disobey your law and do what we want.

You hate our sin but never stop loving us.

Our relationship with you is broken.
All our relations with others are confused.

You hate our sin but never stop loving us.

Forgive us, O God. (FC 11–13)

5

God of everlasting love,
we confess that we have been unfaithful to our covenant with you and
with one another.
We have worshiped other gods: money, power, greed, and convenience.
We have served our own self-interest instead of serving only you and your
people.
We have not loved our neighbor as you have commanded,
nor have we rightly loved ourselves.
Forgive us, gracious God,
and bring us back into the fullness of our covenant with you and one
another. (FC 14–19)

6

God of Abraham, Sarah, and Moses,
we confess that like our mothers and fathers in faith
we have strayed from our covenant with you.
We have worshiped you on Sunday without doing justice throughout the
week.
We have served ourselves before serving you and others.

We have forgotten that we were once slaves whom you rescued,
and we have enslaved others and ourselves.
We have turned away from the lessons of the wilderness
and created new golden calves to worship.
In our wholehearted embrace of the promised land,
a land you gave us,
we have denied a land of promise to others.
Forgive our waywardness and our unfaithfulness
to your promises and our covenant vows.
Restore us, O God, to the fullness of your promise. (FC 14–19)

7

(May be used with Call to Confession #6 and Declaration of Forgiveness #7.)

God of grace,
we confess that we have
elevated the things of this world above you.
We have made idols of possessions and people
and used your name for causes
that are not consistent with you and your purposes.
We have permitted our schedules to come first
and have not taken the time to worship you.
We have not always honored those who guided us in life.
We have participated in systems
that take life instead of give it.
We have been unfaithful in our covenant relationships.
We have yearned for, and sometimes taken, that which is not ours,
and we have misrepresented others' intentions.
Forgive us, O God,
for the many ways we fall short of your glory.
Help us to learn to live together according to your ways. (FC 18)

8

God of mercy and of justice,
we confess that we have not involved our whole heart in loving you.
    We have been stingy in our affections.
We confess that we have not engaged our minds in service to you.

We have allowed others to influence us;
we have forgotten that knowing you means knowing ourselves.
We confess that we have not always loved you
  with the strength that you deserve and our faith demands.
  We have come to believe that the way of faith should always be easy.
We confess that we have loved neither our neighbor nor ourselves.
  We find too many ways to deny our kinship with others
  and too few ways to deny ourselves the things that bring us harm.
Forgive the error of our ways
and bring us back into loving relationship with you
and with one another. (FC 19–20)

DECLARATIONS OF FORGIVENESS

1

Children of God,
Hear the good news:
By grace, God's free gift of love, our sins are forgiven.

But we do not deserve and cannot earn that love.

Such is the nature of God's love and grace.
Children of God,
Believe the good news:
In Jesus Christ your sins are forgiven. **Amen.** (FC 2–3)

2

Although we have turned away from God, God has not turned away from us.
Instead, God sent Jesus Christ to restore our broken humanity.
Jesus lived completely for God, giving himself for our sakes,
  even to the point of dying for us. (SC 21)
In Jesus Christ we are forgiven, and by grace
we are invited to live a life of faith,
conforming our lives to Christ's life,
forgiving others as we have been forgiven.
And so, through Christ, the image of God is now restored.

Thanks be to God!

3

How does God deal with us as sinners?

God hates our sin but never stops loving us. (FC 13)
God's son Jesus sacrificed his life for us by dying on the cross.
He showed his victory over death by rising from the dead.
He removed our guilt and gave us new,
unending life with God. (FC 27)

Children of God, believe the good news:

In Jesus Christ we are forgiven.
Thanks be to God!

4

How does God deal with us as sinners?

God hates our sin but never stops loving us. (FC 13)

What did God do to help us?

**God chose the people of Israel to make a new beginning.
They received God's covenant and prepared the way
for Jesus to come as our Savior.** (FC 14)

How did Jesus prove to be our Savior?

**He sacrificed his life for us by dying on the cross.
He showed his victory over death by rising from the dead.
He removed our guilt and gave us new, unending life with God.** (FC 27)

Children of God, believe the good news:

**In Jesus Christ we are forgiven.
Thanks be to God!**

5

What comfort do you receive from the good news of God's forgiveness?

**That I belong to my faithful Savior Jesus Christ,
who died and rose again for my sake,
so that nothing will ever separate me from God's love.** (FC 36)

Hear the good news!
I declare to you in the name of Jesus Christ,
You are forgiven.

6

(May be used with Call to Confession #5 and Unison Prayer of Confession #5 above.)

God is faithful.

We know this through the biblical witness: God led Israel out of slavery in Egypt, gave them the Ten Commandments through Moses, and brought them into the land that God promised. Even when they, and we, have difficulty remaining faithful, God is always faithful and brings us back to the covenant.

What did God do to bring Israel back to the covenant?

Although God judged the people when they sinned, God still loved them and remained faithful to them. God sent them prophets, priests, and kings. And at last, God promised to send the Messiah.

Friends, believe the good news! It is in the name of the Messiah that all our unfaithfulness and sins are forgiven.
Hallelujah! Amen. (FC 21)

7

Who is in a position to deny us the covenant?
Only God, and God gave us prophets to speak the Word,
God gave us priests to make sacrifices for our sins,
God gave us kings to protect the needy and guarantee justice,
and God gave us the Messiah to forgive our sins at last and restore us, forever,
    to the everlasting covenant of grace.
Friends, believe the good news!
In Jesus Christ, the new covenant, our sins are forgiven. **Amen**. (FC 21)

8

The apostle Paul tells us in Romans, "Therefore, since we are justified by faith, we have peace with God through our Lord Jesus Christ,
through whom we have obtained access to this grace in which we stand" (5:1–2a).

Friends, hear the good news! In Jesus Christ our sins are forgiven.
Amen and Alleluia! (FC 23)

PRAYERS FOR ILLUMINATION

1

Eternal God,
Your Spirit inspired those who wrote the Bible
and enlightens us to hear your Word fresh each day.
Help us to rely always on your promises in Scripture.
In Jesus' name we pray. Amen.

2

Empowering God,
we pray that you will send your Holy Spirit
to move us to understanding;
help us to believe the gospel;
give us strength and wisdom to live by it. Amen. (FC 34)
(Congregation may sing "Spirit of the Living God," PH 322.)

3

Faithful God,
As we open this book we hear again that you welcome
all who have faith in Jesus into the blessings of the covenant.
Let us listen with new ears so that we renew our commitment to love and
     serve you.
In Jesus' name we pray. Amen. (FC 23)

AFFIRMATIONS OF FAITH

1

I am a child of God.
I belong to God, who loved me even before the creation of all that is.
Even though all of us have turned away from God and fallen into sin,
God never stops loving us. (FC 1–2; SC 3; FC 10, 13)
In the fullness of time, God sent Jesus to be our Messiah—the anointed

one—who rescues us from sin and death.
Jesus called disciples to follow him.
He fed the hungry, healed the sick, blessed children, befriended outcasts,
required people to repent, and forgave their sins.
He taught people not to fear but to trust always in God.
He preached the good news of God's love
and gave everyone hope for new life. (FC 22, 26)
As a result of his life and death and resurrection,
and by the power of the Holy Spirit, we are the church.
We are people who believe the good news about Jesus,
who are baptized, and who share in the Lord's Supper.
Through these means of grace,
the Spirit renews us so that we may serve God in love. (FC 35)
I am a child of God. Thanks be to God!

2

[Based on the first article of the Apostles' Creed.]

(May be used on or near Earth Day.)

We believe in God, the Father Almighty, Maker of heaven and earth.
We believe that God's love is powerful beyond measure.
God not only preserves the world; God continually attends to it.

God commands us to care for the earth
    in ways that reflect God's loving care for us.
We are responsible for ensuring that the earth's gifts
    are used fairly and wisely,
that no creature suffers from the abuse of what we are given,
and that future generations may continue
    to enjoy the abundance and goodness
of the earth in praise to God. (SC 7, 22, 19)
Entrusting ourselves wholly to God's care,
we receive the grace to be patient in adversity,
thankful in the midst of blessing,
courageous when facing injustice,
and confident that no evil may afflict us that God will not turn to our
    good. (SC 23)

3

[Based on the second article of the Apostles' Creed.]

We believe in Jesus Christ, God's only Son, our Lord,
whom God anointed to be the Messiah,
the Savior who would rescue us from sin and death.
Although he was truly human, he was also God with us.
As someone who was human, Jesus shared all our sorrows.
Because he was truly God, he saved us from our sins.
Jesus called disciples to follow him.
Jesus fed the hungry, healed the sick, blessed children,
befriended outcasts, required people to repent, and forgave their sins.
He taught people to trust always in God
and preached the good news of God's love. (FC 22, 24, 26)
Jesus sacrificed his life for us by dying on the cross.
He showed his victory over death by rising from the dead.
After his work on earth was done, Jesus returned
to heaven to prepare a place for us and to rule with God in love.
He will come again in glory.
He remains with us now through the gift of the Holy Spirit. (FC 27, 29)

4

[Based on the third article of the Apostles' Creed.]

We believe in the Holy Spirit, which establishes the holy catholic church.
We are the church: the people who believe the good news about Jesus,
who are baptized, and who share in the Lord's Supper.
Through these means of grace, the Spirit renews us
so that we may serve God in love. (FC 31)
All those who live in union with Christ,
whether on earth or with God in heaven, are saints.
Our communion with Christ makes us members one of another.
As by his death Christ removed our separation from God,
so by his Spirit Christ removes all that divides us from each other.
Breaking down every wall of hostility,
the Spirit makes us, who are many, one body in Christ. (SC 66)
God does not will to be God without us,
but instead grants to us creatures, eternal life.
Communion with Jesus is eternal life itself.
By the Holy Spirit, we are joined to Christ through faith,
and adopted as children, the sons and daughters of God.
Through Christ we are raised from death to new life.
For Christ we shall live to all eternity. (SC 87)

5

What do we believe about God the Creator?

We believe that God created all that is, seen and unseen.
We believe that God made us, male and female, in the image of God.

What do we believe about our relationship with this Creator God?

We believe that we are children of God.
We belong to God, who loves us freely
with a love we do not deserve and cannot earn.

How shall we proclaim our love and thanksgiving to God the Creator?

We shall love and trust God with all our heart,
worship God, love others, and respect what God has created.
In our lives we will reflect God's goodness, wisdom, and love. (FC 1–3,
5–6, 8–9)

6

We believe that we were created to live with God, who desires the prayers
    of our hearts.
Our hearts long for God, for we need God's help and guidance every day.
As Jesus taught us, we call upon God like little children who know
that God cares for them and loves them.
We believe that because Jesus prayed to God as his Father,
we can pray to God in this way. (FC 46, 50)
We believe that all good things come from God.
Even in our most ordinary needs, God cares for us completely.
We believe that when we pray the prayer Jesus taught us,
we are praising God for being able and willing
to do everything we ask in this prayer.
We give ourselves over to God's wise and gracious rule,
because we know that God can be trusted to make all things work
    together for good,
now and forever. (FC 55, 59)

7

We believe that in praying to God as "Our Father in heaven" we are calling upon God like little children who know that God cares for us and
loves us, draws near to us from beyond this world, and hears our prayers.
(FC 50, 52)
    We believe that when we say, "Hallowed be your name," we are pray-
ing that God's name will be honored in all the world and everywhere
treated as holy. (FC 53)
    We believe that when we pray, "Your kingdom come, your will be done,

on earth as in heaven," we are asking God to fulfill God's purpose for the whole world. We also ask God to make us able and willing to accept God's will in all things, and to do our part in bringing about God's purpose. (FC 54)

We believe that we ask God to give us our daily bread because all good things come from God. Even in our most ordinary needs, God cares for us completely. (FC 55)

We believe that when we pray, "Forgive us our sins as we forgive those who sin against us," we are telling God we are sorry, asking God not to hold our sins against us, but to accept us again by grace. Because God has forgiven us, we are then to forgive. (FC 56–57)

We believe that when we ask God to "Save us from the time of trial and deliver us from evil," we are asking God to protect us, especially when we need it most. We pray for God to free us from all desires that would lead us to sin and to shelter us from the powers of evil that may threaten us. (FC 58)

We believe that when we pray, "For the kingdom, the power, and the glory are yours, now and forever," we are praising God for being able and willing to do everything we have asked in this prayer. We give ourselves over to God's wise and gracious rule, because we know that God can be trusted to make all things work together for good, now and forever. (FC 59)

We believe that our "Amen" expresses our complete confidence in God, who makes no promise that will not be kept and whose love endures forever. (FC 60)

8

What do we believe about God's help for us?

We believe that God chose the people of Israel to make a new beginning. They received God's covenant and prepared the way for Jesus to come as our Savior.

What do we believe about this covenant?

We believe that the covenant
is an everlasting agreement between God and Israel.
God called Abraham and Sarah and promised
to bless their family, which was later called Israel.

Through the people of Israel,
God vowed to bless all the peoples of the earth.
God promised to be Israel's God,
and they promised to be God's people.
God vowed to love Israel and to be their hope forever,
and Israel vowed to worship and serve only God. (FC 14–16)

9

We believe that we are God's covenant people—
a people who are called into a special relationship with God
and with one another.
We believe in God who
led Israel out of slavery in Egypt,
gave us the Ten Commandments through Moses,
and brought us into the land that God promised.
We believe that
though some remain faithful,
people too often worship other gods
and do not love each other as God commanded.
We believe in God
who loves us even when we sin,
who sent us the Messiah,
forgives our sins,
and remains faithful always. (FC 17, 20–21)

10

We believe in God,
who gave Moses the Ten Commandments and said,
"I am the Lord your God
who brought you out of the land of Egypt,
out of the house of slavery:

    (1) You shall have no other gods before me.
    (2) You shall not make for yourself an idol.
    (3) You shall not make wrongful use of the name of the Lord your God.
    (4) Remember the Sabbath day and keep it holy.
    (5) Honor your father and your mother.
    (6) You shall not murder.

(7) You shall not commit adultery.
(8) You shall not steal.
(9) You shall not bear false witness against your neighbor.
(10) You shall not covet what is your neighbor's."

**We believe that the Ten Commandments are the law of God
and our guide for faith and practice.** (FC 18)

11

**We believe in God who commands us to love
our Lord with all our heart, with all our mind, and with all our strength.
We believe in God who commands us to love
our neighbor as we do ourselves.
We believe in God
who commands us to love.** (FC 19)

ADDITIONAL AFFIRMATION

(This may be used when both sacraments are celebrated.)

**We are the church:
The people who believe the good news about Jesus,
who are baptized, and who share the Lord's Supper.
Through these means of grace, the Spirit renews us
so that we may serve God in love.** (FC 35)

The Sacraments

The Sacrament of Baptism

1

(May be used as an introduction to the Sacrament of Baptism.)

Why do we baptize?

**Because Jesus instructed his disciples to baptize,
and because Jesus himself was baptized by John in the waters of the river
    Jordan,**

**we celebrate this sacrament among the people whom God has called.
Through baptism, we are adopted and welcomed into God's family.
In these waters, we share in the dying and rising of Jesus,
who washes away all our sins.
We are made one with Christ and one with all who are joined
to Christ in the church.** (FC 42)

So let us remember with joy our own baptism even as we celebrate this sacrament today. (FC 40)

2

(May be incorporated into the liturgy for Baptism.)

What is Baptism?

Through baptism I am adopted and welcomed into God's family.
In the water of baptism I share in the dying and rising of Jesus,
who washes away my sins.
I am made one with him and with all who are joined to him in the church.
(FC 42)

Why are we baptized in the name of the Father, and of the Son, and of the
Holy Spirit?

Because of the command Jesus gave to his disciples.
After he was raised from the dead, he appeared to them, saying:
"Go . . . and make disciples of all nations,
baptizing them in the name of the Father and of the Son and of the
    Holy Spirit." (Matt. 28:19, FC 43)

What is the meaning of this name?

It is the name of the Holy Trinity.
The Father is God,
the Son is God,
and the Holy Spirit is God.
And yet they are not three gods, but one God in three persons.
We worship God in this mystery. (FC 44)

3

(May be used as an introduction to Baptism.)

What did God do to help us?

God chose the people of Israel to make a new beginning.
They received God's covenant.

In Baptism we are graced with a new beginning.
Baptism is a sign and seal of God's covenant of grace still with us today.

What is the covenant?

**The covenant is an everlasting agreement between God and God's
   people.**

In Baptism we are engrafted into the family of God.
It is a relationship that endures for a lifetime and beyond.
How did God keep the covenant?

**God led Israel out of slavery in Egypt,
gave them the Ten Commandments through Moses,
and brought them into the land that God had promised.**

In Baptism we are marked as Christ's own; it is a visible sign of God's con-
tinuing faithfulness and a proclamation of our intention to dwell in covenant
with God and one another. (FC 14–17)

4

(May be used as baptismal liturgy.)

*Children of the church gather near the font. An elder presents the one(s) to be
baptized. The minister welcomes the family presenting their child(ren) for
baptism with these words:*

    Minister: What is a sacrament?

    Children
and Family: **A sacrament is a special act of Christian worship that uses visible signs to present God's grace for us in Jesus Christ.** (FC 41)

    Minister: What is baptism?

    Children
and Family: **We are adopted and welcomed into God's family.** (FC 42)
**Through baptism we are named and claimed as God's chil-
dren.**

    Minister: Today we welcome (*N.*) into God's family, the family into which
we were baptized.

*Minister then asks questions of parents and congregation as prescribed in the
Book of Common Worship.*

Parent(s) of infants and younger children

The minister addresses parents presenting children for baptism with these words:

Do you desire that *N.* and *N.* be baptized?

> *The parent(s)*
> *respond:* **I do.**

>> Minister: Relying on God's grace,
>>   do you promise to live the Christian faith,
>>   and to teach that faith to your child?

> *The parent(s)*
> *respond:* **I do.**

Sponsors (if any are present)

The minister addresses the sponsors, if any are present, with these words:

Do you promise, through prayer and example,
to support and encourage *N.*
to be a faithful Christian?

> *The sponsors*
> *respond:* **I do.**

Congregation

The minister addresses the congregation with these words:

Do you, as members of the church of Jesus Christ,
promise to guide and nurture *N.* and *N.*
by word and deed, with love and prayer,
encouraging *them* to know and follow Christ
and to be faithful *members* of his church?

> *The people*
> *respond:* **We do.**

PROFESSION OF FAITH

Through baptism we enter the covenant God has established.
Within this covenant God gives us new life,
guards us from evil,

and nurtures us in love.
In embracing that covenant, we choose whom we will serve
by turning from evil
and turning to Jesus Christ.

*The minister then asks the following questions of the candidates for baptism
and/or the parents or guardians of children being presented for baptism:*

As God embraces you within the covenant, I ask you
to reject sin,
to profess your faith in Christ Jesus,
and to confess the faith of the church,
the faith in which we baptize.

Renunciations
The minister continues, using one of the following:

1

Trusting in the gracious mercy of God,
do you turn from the ways of sin
and renounce evil and its power in the world?

I do.

Do you turn to Jesus Christ
and accept him as your Lord and Savior,
trusting in his grace and love?

I do.

Will you be Christ's faithful disciple,
obeying his Word and showing his love?

I will, with God's help.

2

Do you renounce all evil
and powers in the world
which defy God's righteousness and love?

I renounce them.

Do you renounce the ways of sin
that separate you from the love of God?

I renounce them.

Do you turn to Jesus Christ
and accept him as your Lord and Savior?

I do.

Will you be Christ's faithful disciple,
obeying his Word and showing his love
to your life's end?

I will, with God's help.

3

Trusting in the gracious mercy of God,
do you turn from the ways of sin
and renounce evil and its power in the world?

I do.

Who is your Lord and Savior?

Jesus Christ is my Lord and Savior.

Will you be Christ's faithful disciple,
obeying his Word and showing his love?

I will, with God's help.

Profession

The minister continues:
With the whole church,
let us confess our faith.

Do you believe in God, the Father almighty?

I believe in God, the Father almighty,
creator of heaven and earth.

Do you believe in Jesus Christ?

I believe in Jesus Christ, God's only Son, our Lord,
who was conceived by the Holy Spirit,
born of the Virgin Mary,
suffered under Pontius Pilate,
was crucified, died, and was buried;
he descended to the dead.
On the third day he rose again;
he ascended into heaven,
he is seated at the right hand of the Father,
and he will come to judge the living and the dead.

Do you believe in the Holy Spirit?

I believe in the Holy Spirit,
the holy catholic church,
the communion of saints,
the forgiveness of sins,
the resurrection of the body,
and the life everlasting. Amen. (BCW, pp. 405–409)

> Minister: Why do we use water?
>
> Children
> and family: **In the water of baptism we share in the dying and rising of**
> **Jesus, who washes away our sins.**
>
> Minister: So baptism is like a holy bath.

Minister pours water into the font and offers the prayer of thanksgiving over
the water.

4

(When children are baptized who are not old enough to make their profession of faith, but who are beginning to understand that God loves them, the following questions may be asked of them after the questions to the parents presenting them for baptism.)

Minister: Who are you?

Child(ren): **I am a child of God.** (FC 1)

Minister: What does it mean to be a child of God?

Child(ren): **That I belong to God, who loves me.** (FC 2)

Minister: When we baptize, we show that all of us are children of God and the Spirit seals us in God's love.

5

(May be used as the welcome of the newly baptized and introduction to the congregation.)

Today, in this baptism, we have witnessed a sign of God's everlasting covenant between us, as children of God, and God. This child is a descendant of Abraham and Sarah through the covenant of grace—a blessing to this family, a blessing to our church family, and a blessing to the whole family of creation. Let us rejoice that God is faithful and continues the covenant. Let us welcome [*name*] into the family of God. (FC 15–16)

A LITURGY FOR CELEBRATING A REAFFIRMATION OF BAPTISMAL COVENANT

Many congregations present a baptismal candle to infants and children when they are baptized. The candle may be lit on a child's birthday or the anniversary of the baptismal date as a way of remembering and rejoicing in one's baptism. The following is a suggestion for a rite that can be used in the home, during a church school class, or on some other appropriate occasion.

Parent (or leader, adult) may light the baptismal candle and then say:
When we were baptized, we were clothed with Christ. With our eyes, we see how different we are: male and female, dark skin and light, young and old. Now that we are baptized, in God's eyes we are all dressed to look like Jesus the Christ.

Child: **We are all made in the image of God.** (FC 8)

Parent: When we were baptized, we were made one with Christ, and joined with all who are part of his church.

Child: **When I was baptized I was welcomed into God's family.** (FC 42)

Scripture Readings: *Matthew 28:16–20, Mark 1:9–11, Mark 10:13–16, John 3:1–6, Ephesians 4:4–6, Galatians 3:27–28 are appropriate texts that may have been used during a baptism and may be read aloud in this setting.*

Parent: You were baptized in the name of the Father, Son, and Holy Spirit.

Child: **Because that is what Jesus told his disciples.** (FC 43)

The child may be invited to touch some water to his or her forehead and make the sign of the cross; a prayer may follow.

Dear God: We remember our baptism and give you thanks.
The water reminds us that in the beginning
you tamed the waters of chaos and made everything that is.
The water reminds us that in Jesus Christ we are washed clean and
     forgiven of all our sins.
In spite of all we do wrong, God loves us still. (FC 4)
The water reminds us that the church is our ark.
Like Noah's family and the animals on board,
     we are kept safe in God's care.
The waters of baptism have brought us to the rainbow of God's love.
In the name of the Father, Son, and Holy Spirit we pray. Amen. (FC 42)

Parent: Who are you?

Child: **I am** _____ (Christian name; that is, the first and middle name)**, a child of God.**

The Sacrament of the Lord's Supper

INVITATIONS TO THE LORD'S TABLE

1

This is the Lord's Table; it is a table of welcome for all God's children,
a table that makes visible God's free gift of love,
a love we do not deserve, but a love God wants to give us.
Come, children of God, to the table set by God,
who loves us before we earn that love and in spite of all that we do wrong.
Come taste and know the grace and love of God. (FC 1, 3, 4)

2

This invitation and the first Great Thanksgiving prayer below contain questions and answers on the pattern of the Passover Seder. Children may be invited to join the celebrant at the table; they will need to rehearse before worship so that they may become acquainted with the rhythm of the prayer.

Celebrant: This is the joyful feast of the people of God.

Men: **We have come from east and west.**

Women: **We have come from north and south**

All: **to feast at our Lord's table.**

Celebrant: When our risen Lord was at the table with his disciples,
he took bread and blessed it and broke it and gave it to them.
Then their eyes were opened and they recognized him.

Children: **Who can come to this table?**

Celebrant: Our Savior invites all those who trust him to come to this table.

GREAT THANKSGIVING

1

Celebrant: The Lord be with you.

People: **And also with you.**

Celebrant: Lift up your hearts.

People: **We lift them to the Lord.**

Celebrant: Let us give thanks to the Lord our God.

People: **It is right to give our thanks and praise.**

Children: Why do we give thanks at this table?

People: **We give thanks for God's creation,
for making us in God's image.
We give thanks because God never gave up on us,
even though we were not faithful to God.
We give thanks because when it was time,
God sent the only Son, Jesus, to show God's love for us.**
(FC 7, 8, 13, 23)

Children: How do we praise God for all this?

Celebrant: With all the faithful of every time and place,
we sing this song to God's glory:

People: **Holy, holy, holy Lord, God of power and might.
Heaven and earth are full of your glory.
Hosanna in the highest.
Blessed is he who comes in the name of the Lord.
Hosanna in the highest.**

(A Sanctus familiar to the congregation may be sung. Another variation is
"Santo, Santo," *Lift Up Your Hearts,* 47)

Children: What do we remember at this table?

People: **We remember God's Son, Jesus:**

Women: **He healed the sick and restored sight to the blind;**

Men: **he welcomed strangers and ate with outcasts.**

People: **Dying on the cross, he saved us from our sin,
Risen from the dead, he gives us new life.** (FC 26–27)

Children: Why do we eat bread at this table?

Celebrant: Jesus took bread, blessed it, and gave it to his friends.

Children: Why do we drink from the cup at this table?

Celebrant: Jesus gave them the cup as the promise that our sins are forgiven.

Children: But this is just everyday bread and grape juice.

Celebrant: Let us pray that the everyday bread and juice will become holy:
Gracious God, pour out your Holy Spirit upon us
And upon these your gifts of bread and wine
That the bread we break and the cup we bless
May be the communion of the body and blood of Christ. (FC 45)

People: **Through Christ, with Christ, in Christ,
In the unity of the Holy Spirit,
All glory and honor are yours,
Almighty Father, now and forever. Amen.**

Celebrant: Together let us pray the family prayer that Jesus taught us:

People: **Our Father . . .**

2

Children: What is special about this table?

Celebrant: This is the table of God's family. (FC 45)

Children: What do we celebrate at this table?

Congregation: **We celebrate God's love and faithfulness to us.** (FC 21)

Celebrant: Eternal God, we give you thanks that long ago you promised by the covenant to be our God.
Though some remained faithful to your covenant, we too often worshiped other gods and did not love each other as you commanded.
We all disobey your law.
Although you judge us when we sin,
you still love us and remain faithful to us. **Amen.** (FC 20–21)

Children: What do we remember at this table?

People: **We remember that God sent Jesus to be our Savior and Lord.** (FC 28)

Celebrant: Gracious God, we thank you that Jesus sacrificed his life for us by dying on the cross. He showed his victory over death by rising from the dead. Because of him, we now have new, unending life with you. **Amen.** (FC 27)

Children: Why do we eat bread at this table?

People: **We eat bread at this table because before he died,
Jesus gave bread to his disciples and said,
"This is my body, which is given for you.
Do this in remembrance of me."** (Luke 22:19b)

Children: Why do we drink the cup from this table?

People: **We drink wine because at that same meal, Jesus gave his disciples the cup and said, "This cup that is poured out for you
is the new covenant in my blood."** (Luke 22:20)

Children: What happens as we share the bread and wine?

People: **Jesus renews our faith and gives us the gift of eternal life.
As we remember that he died for us,
we feed on him in our hearts by faith with thanksgiving.**
(FC 45)

Celebrant: Holy God, pour out your Holy Spirit on us
and on these gifts of bread and cup
that we may be renewed to serve you in love.
Send us into the world to proclaim the gospel and
to work for justice and peace. (FC 35, 38)
Through Christ, in Christ, in the unity of the Holy Spirit,
all glory and honor are yours, Almighty God. **Amen.**

3

The Lord be with you.

And also with you.

Lift up your hearts.

We lift them to the Lord.

Let us give thanks to the Lord our God.

It is right to give our thanks and praise.

It is right to praise you, O God.
In the beginning you created all that is, seen and unseen.
You made us, male and female,
and intend that we should reflect your goodness, wisdom, and love. (FC 7–9)
Merciful God, we confess that time and again
we have turned away from you and fallen into sin.
Our relationship with you is broken, and our relations with others are
    confused.
Still, you have never stopped loving us. (FC 10, 12, 13)

So we are bold to raise our voices with the faithful of every time and place,
who forever sing to the glory of your name:

Holy, holy, holy Lord, God of power and might.
Heaven and earth are full of your glory.
Hosanna in the highest.
Blessed is he who comes in the name of the Lord.
Hosanna in the highest.

Almighty God, in times past you sent us prophets to speak your Word,
priests to make sacrifices for our sins,
and kings to protect the needy and guarantee justice.
In this last time, you have sent us the Messiah, Jesus Christ. (FC 21–22)
When Jesus spoke, he spoke with your authority.
When Jesus acted, he acted with your power.
He called disciples to follow him.
He fed the hungry, healed the sick, blessed the children,
befriended outcasts, required people to repent, and forgave their sins.
Jesus preached the good news of your love
and gave everyone hope for new life.
Jesus sacrificed his life for us by dying on the cross.
He showed his victory over death by rising from the dead.
He removed our guilt and gave us new, unending life with you, O God.
(FC 25–27)
Great is the mystery of the faith we proclaim:

Christ has died, Christ is risen, Christ will come again.

As we gather for the Lord's Supper, we are fed at the table of your family.
We ask for the blessing of the Holy Spirit,
that through the bread we eat and the cup we drink,
we may recognize it is our Lord who offers us his body and blood.
Through Christ, we pray, renew our faith and give us the gift of eternal life.
As we remember that Christ has died for all,
may we feed on him in our hearts, by faith, and in thanksgiving. (FC 45)
We were created to live with you, O God.
Our hearts long for you, for we need your help and guidance every day. (FC 46)
So we pray together as Jesus taught his followers to pray:

Our Father . . .

PRAYERS OF THE PEOPLE

1

Petitions may begin with the following:
Loving God, your Spirit gathers us to worship, builds us up in faith, hope, and love, and sends us into the world to proclaim the gospel and to work for justice and peace. (FC 38) Hear our prayers for others and ourselves.

After each petition the following response may be said by all:

Lord, in your goodness, hear our prayer.

2 (introduction to prayers)

Why do we pray to God?

**We pray because we were created to live with God,
who desires the prayers of our hearts.
Our hearts long for God, for we need God's help and guidance every day.**
(FC 46)

Let us join our hearts in prayer.

3

Almighty and loving God,
The world is filled with messages about who we are to be,
how we are to act, and what we are to desire.
Ground us in your Word.
Fill us with a firm and certain knowledge that we are your children,
that you love us and give your gift of grace to us.
We pray for those who have no voice to listen to but their own and the world's.
We pray for children who live in places that do not show your love for them,
for adults who do not reflect your goodness, wisdom, and love,
for an earth that has too often suffered from disrespect.
Empower us to show your love in the world,
to worship you in word and deed,
to love others as you would have us do,
to respect all that you have created.
As people gathered by your Spirit, may our lives proclaim that you love us
not because of what we can do, buy, barter, or earn,
but because we are your children. (FC 1, 3, 6, 9) **Amen.**

4

Eternal God,
Throughout the ages you have shown your love for your people.
When we turned from you, you called us back again and again.
Help us to return to you once more and live as your children,
loving you with our whole heart, mind, and strength,
and loving our neighbors as much as we love ourselves.

You never stop loving us. Thank you, God.

Merciful God,
You called us as your covenant people
and gave us the commandments to show us how to live.
Help us remember the covenant, open our hearts to you,
and obey your law.

You never stop loving us. Thank you, God.
(FC 9, 12, 14–15, 18–19)

Loving God,
By your Spirit, build us up in faith, hope, and love:
faith that we be steadfast; hope that we may never give up;
and love that we may serve the hungry, poor, and suffering.
Send us into the world to work for justice and peace. (FC 38)

You never stop loving us. Thank you, God.

Generous God,
All good things come from you.
Even in our most ordinary needs, you care for us completely.
Help us to reach out to others so they will know that you care for them.
(FC 55)

You never stop loving us. Thank you, God.

(Other petitions may be added.)

5

Mother Father God,
We are more likely to pray for ourselves than for others.
We turn our hearts to the needs of your children.
We pray for the hungry who need bread,
the homeless who need a roof,
the oppressed who need justice,
and the lonely who need fellowship.
Grant hope to the hopeless, grant forgiveness to the sinners,
and empower us to proclaim your gospel to the world. (SC 65)

God of goodness, wisdom, and love,
help us to reach out and touch others with your mercy. (FC 9)
We pray in Jesus' name. **Amen.**

6

God of Israel, God of the covenant, and God of our lives,

Hear us as we pray.

For the many ways in which you kept the covenant:
calling Abraham and Sarah,
blessing their family,
blessing all the peoples of the earth,
leading Israel out of slavery,
giving them the Ten Commandments,
bringing them into the promised land,

We give you thanks.

For the many ways in which you keep the covenant:
calling us to be your disciples,
blessing our families and our lives,
blessing our nation and our world,
leading us away from ways that enslave us,
giving us teaching to follow;
bringing us to a land abundant with promise,

We give you thanks.

Giving God,
Grant that where we are called, we may faithfully serve;
we may be a blessing to those whose names we know and whose faces we
    love;
we may extend that blessing to people we will never know or see.
Where there is oppression and bondage,
grant that we may be instruments of your freedom,
so that all peoples may live according to your desire,
and that all your children, young and old,
may have equal opportunity and access to a land of promise.

We ask these things in the name of Jesus the Christ—the new covenant. Amen. (FC 16–18)

7

Faithful God,
We come to you this day
thankful for our covenant relationship
with you and with one another.
We know that although we have not always been faithful,
you have remained true to your promises.
You send us prophets to speak your word.
Help us to heed what they say and adjust our ways
according to your Word and ways.
You give us priests who minister in the ways of Christ,
who was sacrificed for our sin.
Help us to live in grateful thanksgiving
for the gift of that redemption.
You call leaders and governments
to protect the needy and guarantee justice.
Help us to participate in the process of governing with voices and votes
that hold our governments to God's highest standard of justice and mercy.
You sent the Messiah—Jesus the Christ,
who inaugurated your reign and who promises to return.
Help us to live in covenant community
so that we may embody your kingdom
and be agents of transformation here on earth
until Christ comes again. **Amen.** (FC 21)

8

(This responsive setting of the Lord's Prayer may be offered by a worship leader with congregational response, or the congregation may read it antiphonally.)

Our Father [Parent] in heaven,

We call upon you like little children who know that you care for us and love us.
Draw near to us from beyond this world and hear our prayers. (FC 50, 52)

Hallowed be your name.

We pray that your name will be honored in all the world and everywhere treated as holy. (FC 53)

Your kingdom come, your will be done, on earth as in heaven.

We ask you to fulfill your purpose for the whole world and to make us able and willing to accept your will in all things, and to do our part in bringing about your purpose. (FC 54)

Give us today our daily bread.

All good things come from you. Even in our most ordinary needs, you care for us completely. (FC 55)

Forgive us our sins as we forgive those who sin against us.

We are sorry when we sin. We ask you not to hold our sins against us, but to accept us again by grace. Because you have forgiven us, we know we are then to forgive others. (FC 56–57)

Save us from the time of trial and deliver us from evil.

Protect us, O God, especially when we need it most. Free us from all desires that would lead us to sin, and shelter us from the powers of evil that may threaten us. (FC 58)

For the kingdom, the power, and the glory are yours now and forever.

We praise you, O God, that you have the power to do everything we have asked in this prayer. We give ourselves over to your wise and gracious rule, because we know that you can be trusted to make all things work together for good, now and forever. (FC 59)

We express our complete confidence in you, our God. You make no promise that will not be kept, and your love endures forever. (FC 60) **Amen.**

CHARGES AND BLESSINGS

1

The work of our hands—nurture and strength

In the image of God we are made male and female.

The work of our minds—imagination and reason

In the image of God we are made male and female.

The work of our hearts—compassion and might

In the image of God we are made male and female.

Go forth into the world God created, reflecting through the work of your hands, minds, and hearts the goodness, wisdom, and love of God. (FC 8–9)

2

(May be used in Easter to accompany John 21:15–19.)

Children of God, do you love the One who created you?

We do love you, O God, and will worship you.

Children of God, do you love the One who created you?

We do love you, O God, and will love others.

Children of God, do you love the One who created you?

We do love you, O God, and will respect what you have created.

May God bless you and encourage you in all that you do. (FC 6)

3

The Spirit gathers us to worship God,
builds us up in faith, hope, and love,
and sends us into the world to proclaim the gospel
and to work for justice and peace. (FC 38)

(Congregation may sing "Canto de Esperanza" ["Song of Hope"], PH 432.)

4

Go from this place praising God,
who sends us into the world
to proclaim the gospel and to work for justice and peace.
Give yourselves over to God's wise and gracious rule,
knowing that God can be trusted to make all things work together for good,
now and forever. (FC 35, 59)

5

Go, children of God, out into this world,
living your lives as full members of the covenant,

worshiping and serving only God,
loving each other as God commanded, and
witnessing to God's faithfulness
and transforming love in Jesus the Christ. (FC 16, 20–21)

6

Descendants of Abraham and Sarah,
citizens of the covenant of grace,
go out into this world that God created,
living your lives
as if you are a blessing to both neighborhood and nation,
as if God commanded you to love one another, and
as if the covenant lives on through you . . .
for you are, God has, and it does. (FC 16, 20)

Chapter 2

Proclamation

Preaching the Catechisms

The First Catechism begins with a basic question about the meaning and purpose of life, collectively and individually: "Who are you?" It is not as eloquent or poetic as the Westminster Catechism: "What is the chief end of man?" Nor is the answer as memorable: ". . . to glorify God and to enjoy him forever." (BC 7.001)

The First Catechism, however, asks and answers the question in a simple and direct fashion appropriate for children and for a less eloquent age: "Who are you? I am a child of God." It is a clear truth—the kind of truth that is "like the nose on your face: near at hand and easily discernible but can make you dizzy if you try to focus on it hard" (Garrison Keillor, *We Are Still Married*, N.Y.: Viking, 1989, p. 217).

The question is built for baptismal sermons and is based on some basic baptismal texts from Galatians: "As many of you as were baptized into Christ have clothed yourselves with Christ" (3:27) and, "Because you are children, God has sent the Spirit of his Son into our hearts. . . . So you are no longer a slave but a child, and if a child then also an heir, through God" (4:6–7).

As baptized Christians, we grow to understand that water is thicker than blood. Baptism creates a new family in which all the gathered understand our relationship as brothers and sisters. Mark Searle, the late Roman Catholic author and educator, tells of a conversation with his young son. Searle had just disciplined his six-year-old, and the punishment was not being received graciously. The little boy looked at this father and said: "I wish we were in church right now!" Searle asked, "Why?" Came the reply: "Because in church, you're not the boss of me. In church, you are my brother" (Eleanor Bernstein and John Brooks-Leornard, eds., *Children in the Assembly of the Church*, Chicago: Liturgy Training Publications, 1992, p. 43).

It is fitting that the first thing we affirm as the people of God is that each of us and all of us are children of God. It is a profession that affects not only our relationship with God, but also our relationship with one another.

The first six questions of Belonging to God: A First Catechism form the foundation of Christian stewardship through our theological identity as both God's beloved children and sinners in need of redemption. The catechism introduces us to the inexplicable love of God and the only appropriate human response: gratitude and love. How do we love God? "By worshiping God, by loving others, and by respecting what God has created." (FC 6)

Below are brief reflections on the major themes of the Study Catechism, together with some suggestions for preaching. Although *Belonging to God* has a somewhat different structure, the relevant questions from the First Catechism will be noted in each thematic section.

After the thematic outline of the Study Catechism, a section titled "Proclaiming the Word" follows, with several stories suitable for incorporation into a larger sermon or for telling separately. Each has accompanying commentary with links to the relevant questions from the catechisms.

Identity—Who Am I?

Questions 1–27 in The Study Catechism (see FC 1–6) focus on the questions of Christian identity. The first question, like many other Reformation era catechisms, reflects on the meaning of life: "What is God's purpose for your life?" The response reflects the Pauline formula used in the Brief Statement of Faith: "God wills that I should live by the grace of the Lord Jesus Christ, for the love of God, and in the communion of the Holy Spirit." (SC 1)

Question 5 specifically asks what a Christian believes and offers the response that basic beliefs may be found in the Apostles' Creed. Questions 6–27 (SC) speak to the first article, namely, that Christians believe in God, the Father Almighty. Question 7 specifically identifies God as a God of love whose love is "powerful beyond measure." Themes of the stewardship and care for the natural world are lifted up in Question 19, which insists that "no creature should suffer from the abuse of what we are given." The contemporary nature of the catechism is evident in Question 24, in which Christian faith meets the pain and despair of the human psyche.

Christology

Questions 28–48 (SC; see FC 22–29) deal specifically with Jesus and the second article of the Apostles' Creed. Questions 29 and 30 speak of the unique person and work of Jesus Christ, whereas Questions 32–35 address the paradox of a Christ who is truly human and truly God.

World Religions

Questions 49–52 (SC) address the pluralism of our modern age. Taking off from the image of Christ as the one who will judge the living and the dead, the catechism asks if all human beings will be saved. The catechism holds up the unique truth contained in the gospel of Jesus Christ while counseling hospitality and grace in the company of those who hold other beliefs. "I should always welcome and accept these others in a way that honors and reflects the Lord's welcome and acceptance of me." (SC 52)

Diana Eck, the Harvard professor, has offered a provocative look at the religious landscape in America in her book, *A New Religious America*. In her view, these questions of how Christians, Muslims, Buddhists, Jews, and others will coexist in America are perhaps the most important questions religious people can raise. She describes us as a nation of people who are "afraid of ourselves" and provides illustrations of the many ways that we silence and stigmatize people of different faiths.

In 1999, the oldest synagogue west of the Mississippi River was deliberately burned down and its library of five thousand books destroyed. A mosque in Yuba City, California, was burned down before it was ever completed. In Flint, Michigan—at another mosque—vandals slashed every single tire on the cars in the parking lot while the faithful were at prayer. In Kansas City, the faithful came to their Hindu Temple only to find a side of beef hanging near the altar and the word *Leave* painted in blood on the walls.

Some Christians have responded to such attacks with acts of compassion and financial support. Many more, however, prefer not to get involved. It is noteworthy that The Study Catechism addresses these issues by counseling hospitality. "Welcome one another . . . just as Christ has welcomed you" (Rom. 15:7) is the text cited and used to extol hospitality as the queen of Christian virtues.

Barbara Brown Taylor illustrates the point when she describes attending worship at the Atlanta Masjid of al-Islam a few days after the terrorist attacks of September 11, 2001. The worship leader was Imam Plemon El-Amin, who taught with these words: "The red, white, and blue is good, but it is not good enough. The Qur'an teaches us that the world started out as one and will end as one, with one single soul called humanity."

After the service, Taylor and fifteen students that she brought to the Masjid were surrounded by well-wishers. They were hugged and kissed and welcomed. Taylor tried to apologize because some of the students were not dressed appropriately and they had stumbled many times during the prayers and liturgy, but the congregation would hear nothing of it. "No, no, no," they said. "It is a blessing for us to have you here—because there are so many misconceptions about Islam, but now you have come to see and hear for yourself what we believe."

Taylor writes: "At the end of one of the most divisive weeks any of us had lived through, there was no mistaking who we were: we were children of one God, with one soul called humanity" (Christian Century, Sept. 26—Oct. 3, 2001).

Sin and Forgiveness

Questions 20 and 80–83 in the Study Catechism (see FC 10–13) address issues of human sin and the meaning of forgiveness.

Holy Spirit

Questions 4, 53–55, 59, 67, and 76 in the Study Catechism (see FC 30–34) address the topic of the Holy Spirit. The third article of the Apostles' Creed is a sprawling section of the catechism, Questions 53–88. This section takes several theological turns along the way, reflecting on many contemporary concerns. Questions 66 and 84–88 bring the discussion back to the themes of the Apostles' Creed: communion of saints, resurrection of the body, and life everlasting.

Scripture

Questions 56–61 in the Study Catechism (see FC 37) deal with the Word of God. Modern critical methods of interpreting Scripture are mentioned in Question 61.

The Church and Its Mission

Questions 62–65 in the Study Catechism (see FC 35–38) offer a definition of the church, clarification of the profession that the church is both "holy" and "catholic," and a poetic understanding of how all of us are "needy" in the eyes of God. The Study Catechism asks provocative questions for proclaiming the gospel to children. Question 65 asks, "Who are the needy?" and Question 88 asks, "Won't heaven be a boring place?" A traditional folktale called "Once a Good Man" offers a story that connects these two questions—and bridges images of heaven and earth as well. The story may be found in *The Hundredth Dove and Other Tales,* by Jane Yolen (Schocken Books).

Sacraments

Baptism is the subject of Questions 71–76 in the Study Catechism (see FC 42–44); the Lord's Supper is addressed in Questions 77–79 in the Study Catechism (see FC 45); sacraments in general are discussed in Questions 67–70 in the Study Catechism (see FC 41).

Spiritual Disciplines—A Rule of Life

The Study Catechism presents the Ten Commandments as a rule for life: "They teach us how to live rightly with God and one another." (SC 89) Questions 89–119 offer a summary and interpretation of the commandments (see FC 18–19).

Prayer

The last section of the Study Catechism, Questions 120–134, focuses on prayer, and specifically the Lord's Prayer. Question 120 offers a description of the many forms and purposes of prayer (see FC 46–60).

Proclaiming the Word

1

THEME: LIFE OF JESUS—CHRISTIAN LIFE

The First Catechism asks a number of relevant questions for newly initiated Christians (usually children, in our Presbyterian tradition). Question 24 asks, "Was Jesus just another human being?" and we hear an answer that describes how Jesus shared human sorrow while saving us from sin. Question 35 asks about the nature of the church, and we hear a reply about a community built up in faith, hope, and love. The following story—a legend concerning the saint of the church known as Valentine—speaks to these two questions, and it also offers a commentary on one of the questions from The Study Catechism: "How shall we treat non-Christians? (SC 52). Valentine responds to the pluralism of his world by being courageous, generous, and faithful.

Valentine lived in ancient Rome almost two thousand years ago. He was a doctor, a humble man who knew how to mix herbs and powders with wine, milk, and honey in order to make medicine that would make people feel better, ease their pain, and heal their illnesses.

Some of Valentine's patients were so poor that they could not pay him, but Valentine did not worry about that. He would say to his patients: "It was but a few herbs and prayer that have healed you, my friend."

Valentine prayed for his patients only at night and only in private, because he lived in Rome during days when it was dangerous to admit that you were a Christian. Christians were often arrested by the Emperor. When there was a disaster like a flood or an earthquake, the Emperor blamed it on Christians— and he had a few of them arrested, thrown in jail, or even killed.

One day a man who was a jailer in the Emperor's prison came to Valentine. When Valentine saw him standing at his door, he was afraid that this jailer had come to arrest him. But that was not why he had come—not at all. The jailer

had a daughter who was blind, and he had come hoping that Dr. Valentine might be able to help his daughter.

Valentine warned the jailer, "There is no guarantee that I can help her, but I will try. I will make an ointment and apply it to her eyes. I will have to see her once a week for many weeks. You will have to apply this ointment every day. But if you are willing to do this, then I am willing to try." The next day, the little girl came, and Valentine put the ointment on her eyes. That night he prayed for her.

This went on for weeks and months—throughout the summer, fall, and winter. As spring came, the girl was still getting treatments from Dr. Valentine. Each week, she and her father went out into the fields and collected the wild spring flowers that were beginning to blossom. Her favorite was the crocus, because of the way it smelled. Even though they could not pay Dr. Valentine for the many treatments he had given her, she brought him flowers every week.

One day, soldiers came to Valentine's home, but they did not come because they needed a doctor. They came to arrest him because he was a Christian.

In jail, the jailer brought Valentine gifts of food and books and some things he needed in order to continue to be a doctor for people. Even in jail, Valentine took care of anyone who asked. Valentine continued to make the ointment for the jailer's little girl, and he applied it to her eyes every day.

Finally, there came a day when Valentine was led away from his jail cell to be killed. There was nothing that even the jailer could do for him. But as he was led away to die, he handed the jailer a little scroll of papyrus—of paper. "It's for your daughter," Valentine told the jailer.

When the jailer returned home that day, he was greeted by his daughter. He slid the scrap of papyrus out of his belt, unrolled it, and handed it to the child.

"What does it say, Father? What does it say?" she asked, as a yellow crocus fell from the small scroll into her hand. "From your Valentine," her father read.

Tears came to the little girl's eyes. Slowly she held up the blossom before her face, and for the first time, she watched its color dazzle like the rays of the rising sun.

COMMENTARY

This story, among the legends told of St. Valentine, works well during the season of Ordinary time following Epiphany, which is normally when Valentine's Day falls. It seems particularly appropriate on Transfiguration Sunday, when the theme of transformed vision is prominent. It can be told with a yellow crocus in hand to help younger children focus. They can be encouraged to smell the flower and see the dazzling color referred to in the story.

People in the story are presented as real people: a humble doctor, a hurting child, a caring father. The miracle is not undercut, but the story focuses on the simple faith of Valentine and the faith that the jailer and daughter had in him, and through him in his God.

At the end of the story, the flower is compared to the rising sun, which is linguistic play that older children may appreciate. The "rising Son" is, of course, the focus of the story, the biblical lesson, and the liturgical season. Younger children will recognize the phrase that is printed on all the hearts of the season, "From your Valentine." Because young children often associate hearts with their faith and their church (God is after all a God of love), the story provides them with a narrative to connect the symbol and the meaning they have already associated with that symbol.

2

THEME: JESUS CHRIST AS LORD

Questions 27–28 in the First Catechism deal with Jesus Christ as our Lord and Savior. The answers, however, remain largely abstract, especially for young children. The following story suggests Easter themes in a contemporary and concrete setting. Death is real, and so is the transforming power of the risen Lord.

There was once a little boy named Phillip. Phillip was born with a condition that made it hard for him to learn and understand. When he was a baby, he looked like other babies; but as he grew older, children were aware that there was something different in the way that Phillip looked and spoke and thought.

Phillip went to Sunday School. Though he could not keep up with his classmates at school and had to stay in first grade when they all went on to higher grades, Phillip was in the same Sunday School class with children his own age. When Phillip turned nine, he was in the nine-year-old class, although everyone else was in the third grade and he remained a first-grader.

You may know something about nine-year-olds. They learned and laughed and played together. They cared about each other in their Sunday School class, and they tried hard to be kind to Phillip, even though they knew something was different. Their teacher knew that Phillip was just not part of the group. Phillip did not choose nor did he want to be different. He just was, and that was the way things were.

When Easter came around, the teacher decided to try something new with his class. He had collected several plastic eggs—you've seen them, I'm sure. On Easter morning, you might have seen them in an Easter basket filled with jelly beans or some other kind of candy. Well, the teacher had enough of these empty plastic eggs to give one to each child in the class. It was a beautiful spring day, and each child was asked to take the egg outside, on the church grounds, and find a symbol for new life, put it into the egg, and then bring it back to the classroom. Then they would mix up all the eggs, open them, and share their new life symbols and surprises with one another, one by one.

Well, they did this, and it was glorious—and confusing! It was wild! They ran all around, gathered their symbols, and returned to the classroom. They put all the eggs on a table, and then the teacher began to open them. All the children were standing around the table, eagerly waiting for the teacher to open their eggs.

He opened an egg and in it was a spring flower. Everyone ooh-ed and aah-ed. Flowers are a sign of new life.

He opened another. There was a little bug inside. Some kids said, "uggh." Others said, "cool." But they all agreed. After the winter, even the coming of bugs is a sign of new life.

Some eggs had grass, some had rocks; one even had a butterfly inside.

Then the teacher opened an egg, and there was nothing there. Someone said, "That's not fair—that's stupid. Somebody didn't do it right."

All the kids were complaining because it seemed that someone did not play the game according to the rules. Then the teacher felt a tug on his shirt, and he looked down to see Phillip standing beside him.

"It's mine," he said. "That one is mine."

Someone said, "It's Phillip's. He doesn't do anything right. There's nothing there."

"I did so do it," Phillip answered back. "And I did it right. Teacher's lesson said that everyone knew about new life because Jesus' tomb was empty. See, my egg is empty—the tomb is empty. New life, right?"

All the confusion and wildness and noise stopped for a minute. There was silence—a very full silence. There are people who don't believe in miracles, so I won't say that what happened that day in the third-grade class full of nine-year-olds was a miracle. But from that time on, things were different in the classroom. It was as if Phillip finally became a part of that group of nine-year-olds. They took him in. He entered. He was set free from the tomb of his different-ness.

Two years later, Phillip died. His family had known from the day he was born that he wouldn't live a full life span. Many things were wrong with his small body. So, late in the summer, with an infection that most children could have easily shrugged off, Phillip died. The mystery of life and death simply enveloped him completely.

At Phillip's funeral, held at his church in Houston, there were ten eleven-year old children who marched up to the table, not with flowers to cover the stark reality of death. Ten eleven-year old children, with their Sunday School teacher, carried empty plastic eggs that usually hold jelly beans, broke them open, and placed them on the table to remind us all that death is past; the victory of new life has been won for us by Jesus Christ, because the tomb is empty. Amen.

COMMENTARY

This story was authored by Harry Pritchett, Jr., in St. Luke's Journal of Theology, *University of the South, Sewanee, Tennessee, Volume XIX, no. 3. It is, however, a story that is by now much traveled, and few would be able to cite this source for the story.*

Although it is somewhat sentimental in nature, drawing too heavily on a young child's death as the source of its pathos, there is a solid theological core to the story. Unlike many Easter stories for children, death is not ignored and new life is not sweet and easy. The story is grounded in a child's real experience and interpreted through Easter light. The scandal of the cross is a part of this story's power.

Because the characters of the story are nine-year-olds attending Sunday School, they are very real to children hearing this story. Phillip's situation is one that children can imagine. They probably have experienced a time when they themselves were in a group, but did not feel part of that group. Preadolescence is often an age when children are acutely aware that they are different from others.

This story should be told with a plastic egg in hand, just in case there are some children who do not know what you are talking about. Young children will respond to some of the classroom banter and will imagine a class period where they might be allowed to run around the grounds of the church. Older children will hear the Easter message in a setting that brings it close in time and space, not just as an event long ago and far away.

3

THEME: GOD'S COVENANT FAITHFULNESS

The First Catechism introduces the idea of God's covenant through Questions 22–23. By sending Jesus, God opened the covenant with Abraham to the whole world. Jesus is the "anointed one"—the Messiah—who would rescue all of us from sin and death. The following story is a Jewish story told for Hanukkah; but for Christian children, it places us, the children of God, in the company of all who look for God to save us from the evil of this world.

This morning I am telling a true story. It happened more than fifty years ago during the days of December. It was the time of year when the world seems dark and damp and cloudy, when days are short and nights are long and cold. People who were alive all those years ago might tell you the whole world was dark in those days. The world was at war, and fear was everywhere.

David and Rebecca lived in the same neighborhood. David was twelve and Rebecca was nine, so they didn't really know each other. They were Jewish children living in Warsaw, Poland. When the war began, they—and all Jewish people, children and adults—were forced to wear yellow stars on their jackets so that all could see that they were Jewish.

Then, one terrible night, the soldiers came to take everyone away to a prison camp. There was shooting and crying and screaming, dogs barking.

Families were separated, houses were burned, windows were shattered. David and Rebecca ran away. Their parents sent them running into the night, told them to hide from the soldiers and to stay hidden. That night they found one another hiding in the rubble that had been their neighborhood.

They found a hiding place, cold and dark and lonely, but away from the dogs and the soldiers and the guns. They stayed there one night, then the next and the next. David would go out at night, when the hiding place was even darker. He found food for them in garbage cans and old clothes to keep them warm.

One night, David came back after looking for food. He had found a treasure: baked potatoes thrown away while they were still warm, dried mushrooms, and a whole chocolate candy bar, still wrapped.

"And look what else," he cried to Rebecca. "I have found an old candle and some matches. I have tried to keep track of the time since we came to this hiding place, and if I am right, tonight is the first night of Hanukkah. Come, you light the first candle of the holiday and we'll celebrate!"

Rebecca lit a candle, and together they said the prayer over the light. It was strange how one little candle lit up their hiding place. They had not really seen each other since they had come there. Now the light revealed their dirty, tear-stained faces, their matted hair and tired eyes. But beneath the exhaustion there was hope that danced in the candlelight as it reflected in their eyes.

The children sat by the light and remembered—remembered happier holidays surrounded by family, opening presents, playing games, telling stories, and singing. They laughed together as each remembered and told a story.

Then Rebecca turned to David. "Let's escape," she said. "Tonight. Let's leave this place and try to find somewhere safe and dry. We don't know what has happened to our parents, and we may never know. But let's save ourselves tonight."

David had been waiting to hear such words from Rebecca. He knew that they would eventually freeze to death or starve in this hiding place. He had planned how to get out of the city, but he would never have left without Rebecca. He needed her to have courage, and this night she had it.

They waited until the candle burned so low that they could hold it no longer. Then they extinguished the light and walked out into the night.

David had planned an escape through the sewers of the city. The water down there would be ice cold. There might be rats, but there would be no soldiers.

This night it was so cold that the sewer water had turned to ice. They could almost skate through the sewers. It was apparently too cold even for the rats, for they did not see any. They made their way to the edge of the city walking under it, in the sewers. When they came up to the street, it was late and all lights were out. It was even too cold for many guards to be out around the city. They escaped unseen, and in the countryside they found a barn with soft, warm hay to sleep in.

In the morning, they discovered that the barn was owned by people known as "partisans." They were people helping Jews escape from Poland and find a home back in the Holy Land, in Israel. Within a few weeks, David and Rebecca were on board one of the first ships sailing from Europe to Israel. In Israel they were greeted by friends. Each of them was given a new home and family. David lived in Jerusalem and Rebecca in Tel Aviv. Each went to school, and when David turned twenty-one and Rebecca was eighteen, they were married.

Now I told you this story was true. I can say that because David and Rebecca told this story to their grandchildren. Each year in December, on the first night of Hanukkah, they tell it again. And when they come to the part about the candle, Rebecca will say: "It was the light that gave us courage. It was the power of light that showed us something that was inside of us that we didn't know we had. In that candlelight was faith and hope and courage and love. We looked at the light and walked out into the world knowing that God was with us."

We Christians do not celebrate Hanukkah, but we do celebrate the light. We know something about the power of light that brings faith, hope, and love into our lives. We believe that Jesus Christ is the light of the world, light for all people. It is that light that we lift up, certain that no darkness will ever overcome it. Amen.

COMMENTARY

This story is adapted from a story told by Isaac Bashevis Singer. Even though it is a story for Hanukkah, that Jewish holiday often falls during Advent. Certainly, there are many Advent themes in this story: light versus darkness, hope versus fear, God's saving love, our human expectation of salvation.

The story is best told with a candle that is lit when Rebecca lights the candle in the story. Then it is extinguished at the end of the story, just before the "Amen." A child may be invited to blow out the candle at the end.

Children today live in a pluralistic world, and many school-age children probably have friends who are Jewish. At school, they will have heard something of the holiday. When the church can communicate that it knows something about the stories and traditions of other faiths, it prepares children to understand that Christian faith interprets not just its own story, but the stories of others as well.

The gospel is in this story in the faithfulness of David and Rebecca and the unnamed God who leads them out of fear and into light. The scandal of the cross is apparent in this story. Older children and teenagers will recognize the scandal of "Christian" soldiers coming to imprison Jewish children. Young children will recognize the darkness and danger and threat of death. Some may even associate the darkness with the darkness that comes over the earth during the crucifixion. Perhaps they will hear the echoes of John's Prologue.

The gospel claim that the light overpowers all darkness is the last word. So with confidence, we blow out the candle in order to walk in the light that Christ has already prepared for us.

4

THEME: JESUS—THE NEW COVENANT/CHRISTMAS

Question 23 of the First Catechism proclaims that "By sending Jesus, God opened up the covenant with Abraham to the whole world." The connection between creation and incarnation has been made through folktale and legend by telling stories about the animals in the stable. Animals that either talk or express sentiment are a part of the seasonal tales told at Christmas, and this story stands in that tradition.

Long ago, in the little mountain villages of the southwestern United States—in towns of New Mexico and Colorado—people did not need watches and clocks and calendars to tell time. They could always tell what time of year it was by the work of Teofillo, the woodcutter, and his donkey.

When the weather was fine and days were sunny, people could see that Teofillo did not work hard. He did not need to cut much wood, so it must be summer. When he spent all his time in the forest cutting wood, it must be fall. People would soon need wood to warm their homes and bake their bread. When the snow came, and Teofillo's burro had his back filled with wood to be delivered to village homes, then it was winter. And the coming of winter meant that Christmas was not far behind.

One year, however, the snows came early and they did not stop. It started snowing in October, and by December snow was piled up halfway over everyone's windows. Teofillo had to cut more and more wood, and his burro had to deliver so much wood that everyone lost track of time. Everyone, that is, except the donkey.

Teofillo's donkey knew that Christmas was coming, but he also could tell that all the people had forgotten. No one was baking; they were not decorat-

ing their homes; there were no Christmas trees, no carol singing, nothing. Now you may wonder how the donkey remembered, but you should know that the one day each year when the donkey did not have to work was Christmas. On Christmas, the donkey got to rest. There would be extra hay to eat and sleep on. And usually at Christmas, Teofillo would bring him a special Christmas treat to eat.

The donkey did not want to miss Christmas, so he gathered all the animals in the barnyard together and told them that Christmas was coming, but the people had forgotten. It was the rooster who came up with a plan. "I know just what to do," the rooster announced, and then he told all the animals his plan. "It will take practice, but we can do it." They all liked the plan.

That night was Christmas Eve. When all the people had gone to sleep, thinking it was just an ordinary night, the animals put their plan into action.

At midnight the church bells struck the hour. Twelve times the bells rang. Then from the top of the steeple, the rooster began to crow. *"Cristooo naciooo!"* *"Cristooo naciooo!"*

Then out on the village square the donkey brayed, *"En Belen . . . En Belen."*

The chickens began clucking all around the yard, *"por que, por que."*

To which the ducks quacked an answer, *"paz, paz, paz."*

Then the cow chimed in, *"amor, amor, amor."*

The people heard all the commotion from their beds, got up and looked out, rubbed their eyes and then their ears.

"It sounds like the animals are talking. What are they saying?"

They were speaking—speaking Spanish, for it was a little Spanish town. This is what the people heard:

Cristo nacio—Christ is born
En Belen—in Bethlehem.
por que—For what?
Paz y amor—For peace and love.

"Christ is born in Bethlehem for peace and love! It must be Christmas! How could we have forgotten?"

So the people threw on their clothes. They started baking and wrapping presents. They started decorating their homes with wreaths and *ristras,* and they set out *farolitos* all over the village to light the way for the Christ Child. Then, just before dawn, the people went to church to pray their prayers and sing carols and give glory to God.

The next day, the people held a feast. When the feast was over, many came out to the barnyard with special treats for the animals who had helped them remember Christmas. I think the people half-expected the animals to say "*gracias*" or at least "*Feliz Navidad.*" But they didn't. There was just grunting and clucking and crowing and braying.

In fact, the people of the village never heard their animals talk again. But then again, the animals never had to, because no one ever forgot Christmas again. And if you were to visit one of those little village churches tonight—this night—on Christmas Eve, you would see on the front of the church bulletin is printed the name of the church service: "*El Missa del Gallo*"—the Mass of the Rooster.

Why the rooster? After all, he did not remember Christmas. He was just the loudest. What about the burro? He was the one who remembered.

Well, don't worry about the burro, for he is honored too. In fact, the next time you see a burro, look on his back. Next time you are at the zoo, or if you go to the nativity at the Festival of Lights, you will see that the burro has a thin strip of black fur running down his gray back and another strip of fur across the shoulders. Yes, the little burro now has the shape of the cross on its back. The burro that would not forget Christmas now forever reminds us all of Christ. So it should be every Christmas, and every time we gather here.

COMMENTARY

This is an old folktale that has been collected by storyteller Joe Hayes. It is one of those explanatory tales ("so that's how the leopard got his spots") that has been given an association with Christmas and the church.

The story is entertaining and playful. Young children delight in the animal noises and the Spanish language. Older children like the nonsense in the story

that comes round to make some sense. They are usually surprised by the rev-
elation regarding the Mass of the Rooster.

There is not much scandal here, but the cross is present, which is rare in
Christmas stories for children. The claim is a bit of a play on words. Though
no one would forget Christmas, even children know that it is easy to forget the
Christ at Christmas. The burro's back is a reminder to us all that there is no
Christmas without the cross.

5

THEME: TRUST

Question 26 of the First Catechism describes Jesus as a teacher, and the tale
that follows is one used by rabbis for centuries as a teaching tool. We know
from the scholarly community that Jesus often taught with humor, though the
humor in many parables is not accessible today, for children or adults. The
catechism indicates that Jesus taught people to "trust in God always," which
is the theme of this story. The result of his teaching is to give everyone hope
for new life, and that is precisely the conclusion of this story. In The Study
Catechism: Confirmation Version, Question 51 asks a poignant question,
"Who are the needy?" The answer offers a poetic description of those with
practical needs as well as spiritual needs. The story that follows features a
character who approaches his rabbi with what he thinks are practical needs.
Notice that the man is presented as one who has "enough." He is not the poor,
so that in the end, when the man receives a spiritual solution for his practical
problems, it is not a less than satisfactory solution. So too, when Jesus
preached to the multitudes, offering them a life free from anxiety, he was not
ignoring the real, practical needs of poor people. This story is presented here
as commentary on a portion of the Sermon on the Mount, Matthew 6:25–33.

Jesus told his disciples, "Why do you worry about what you will eat and what
you will wear? Look at the birds," he says. "God even feeds the birds. Look at
the flowers, they have the best clothing of all! They are worry free. So don't be
anxious; seek God's kingdom first, then everything else will be given to you."

When Jesus said these things, it was not the first time people had heard such
a message. In fact, rabbis have told a similar story for almost as long as we
have told this story of Jesus. Maybe Jesus even heard a similar story from rabbis when he was growing up.

Once there was poor man—well, not so poor, but not so rich either. He had
enough. A table to eat at and food to put upon it, a wife and six good children,
a place to sleep, a small farm to keep.

Then his wife's parents had a fire, and they had no place to go except to his house. The house was already small, the meals were already meager, but soon after his mother-in-law and father-in-law moved in, there seemed to be no room and no peace at all. All the children were suddenly quarrelsome. There was no peace during the day, and at night? Well, you have never heard such snoring.

Finally, the poor man reached the end of his patience. Not knowing what else to do, he came to the rabbi. "Rabbi, you must help me. I haven't had a moment's peace since my in-laws moved in. Now we are all miserable. There is not enough to eat, no room to sleep. There is fighting and snoring. Rabbi, what should I do?"

The rabbi pulled his beard and thought for a while. "Do you have some chickens at home?"

"Yes, I have chickens, but what has that to do with my problem? It's my house, my in-laws that are the problem."

"Go home and take the chickens in the house to live with you."

"All right, Rabbi," though the poor man was a bit surprised.

Of course, when the man brought his chickens into his house, it was not but a few hours before things were much worse. There was less room and more noise. There were feathers everywhere, and the smell from the chickens was terrible. Before a week had passed, the man had lost his patience, so he went back to the rabbi and begged for help.

"Good Rabbi, see what misfortune has befallen me. Now with the crying and quarreling and snoring, there is clucking and crowing and feathers in my soup. Things could not be worse. Help me, Rabbi!"

The rabbi stroked his beard and thought for a while. "You have a goat, don't you?"

"Yes, Rabbi, I have a goat, but what has that to do with my problem? No, you aren't going to suggest . . ."

"Go home and bring the old goat into your house to live with you."

"Rabbi, you can't really mean it."

"I do indeed. Now, go home."

The poor man went home, hanging his head. He brought the goat into the house, and it was not a few minutes before things got much worse. The goat went wild, butting everyone who turned his back, eating anything that he could reach. There was less room and more noise, and no one was sleeping well. When the poor man could no longer stand it, he went back to the rabbi.

"Holy Rabbi, the goat is running wild! My children are terrified! My life is a nightmare!"

The rabbi stroked his beard and thought. "You have a cow, don't you?"

The poor man did not say a word, but silently walked home and brought the cow into the house. Is the rabbi crazy? he wondered.

By now, life in the house was crazy. Even the chickens were quarreling. The goat ran wild, the cow trampled everything. The smell was horrible. There was no peace, night or day. The poor man got up early the next morning to confront the rabbi and tell him that he was crazy.

"Rabbi, save me! Help me! The end of the world has come. There is no room to even breathe, and if you tell me to take one more animal into my house, I will go mad."

The rabbi stroked his beard and thought. "Go home, my son, and let the animals out of your house."

"I will, Rabbi, right away. Thank you, oh, thank you."

The man ran home, opened the doors of his house and sent out the cow, the goat, and all the chickens. The children swept out all the feathers, and his wife cooked a fine meal. That night there was much room around the table, and there seemed to be plenty to eat. No one fought or quarreled. And at night, when all were sleeping, the gentle sound of snoring was like a lullaby to him, sending him into a deep and peaceful sleep.

The very next day, he went back to the rabbi. "Holy Rabbi, you have made life sweet for me. Life couldn't be better. I don't know how you did it, but there is more of everything. I give God the glory, good Rabbi, that God sent you and your wisdom to me." And the man went dancing down the road back home.

The rabbi stood and stroked his beard and thought: "You see, it could always be worse."

COMMENTARY

This is an old rabbinic tale that probably took this form during the eighteenth century in Eastern Europe. There are Hasidic threads of the story that go back even farther.

The gospel message, "Why should you worry?" is given a comic reversal in this story—it could always be worse. The story is delightful for children. It has some traditional elements of storytelling—the repetition of phrases, the anticipation of the rabbi's next answer, the revelation to the poor man that even young children can see coming long before the story concludes.

The story captures some of the tone that may have been present even in Jesus' parables. Surely, the notion that God feeds the birds was a revelation intended to make a first century Palestinian audience laugh as well. The gospel claim that we can live without anxiety in God's kingdom is still present in the story.

6

THEME: THE COVENANT, DAVID AND GOLIATH

Questions 14–21 of the First Catechism deal with the concept of the covenant between God and God's people. In spite of our sin and imperfection, God remains faithful to us, even when we are disobedient. God has called special people to carry the covenant across generations: fathers and mothers in faith, prophets, priests, and kings. "God called kings to protect the needy and guarantee justice," the catechism teaches. (FC 21) The people of Israel received God's covenant and prepared the way for Jesus to come as our Savior (FC 14) The story of David and Goliath hints at the ways in which the covenant stretches across the Old and New Testaments, from King David to Jesus, the Son of David.

Long ago, a man stepped out of his tent holding onto a great horn from a ram. He put the horn to his mouth, and the horn gave a great blast that could be heard for miles across the desert valley.

The people who heard the sound knew it meant danger. A foreign king and his army were invading. The sound of the horn called people to put down their plowshares and take up swords in order to defend their common land. Each family was expected to send at least one young man to fight the invaders.

On the edge of the valley lived a man named Jesse, who sent three of his older sons to the battle. He had faith in his people, his sons, and the God who would protect them. But three days after he had sent his sons to the war front, there was still no word about the fighting.

So Jesse sent for his youngest son, who had stayed home to care for the flocks of sheep and other animals. This son's name was David. Jesse loaded up David with food to send to the battle front—enough food to feed, well, to feed an army. "Give the food to your brothers' commander, and bring me back

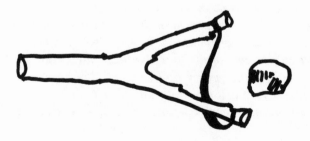

word about the fighting. Don't you stay and try to join in the fight," Jesse said, for he knew that though David was young, David had a reputation as a fighter, a leader among men, and a singer of songs.

When David arrived at the battlefront, he found his brothers and made sure that they and their fellow soldiers were well fed. While they were eating lunch, a huge man came out from among the army of the Philistines. He had to be more than seven feet tall, wearing armor that covered his chest, arms, and legs. He had a helmet so large that one could have taken a bath in it. His shield was so big that it took one man just to carry the shield and nothing else. His spear was described as being as big around as a weaver's beam and at least six feet long.

This "Goliath" of a man called out to the army of Israel: "Why won't anyone come out and fight me? Come, send just one soldier. We don't all need to fight. Just your best soldier against me, one on one. If your soldier wins, we will all be your slaves. If I win, then we will make all of Israel our slaves. So come on. Is there no one in this land brave enough to fight me?"

When David heard this speech, he asked his brothers, "Who is this dog that calls out like this against Israel? Do you let him talk this way every day without fighting him?"

"Surely, little brother, you see his size? Who would want to go out and fight such a giant? We call him Goliath, and there is no one to challenge him. Now go on home and tell our father that the fighting goes well."

But David was angry, and he said, "I will fight this Goliath!" His brothers tried to convince him to go home, but David could not be stopped. King Saul—the man who had blown the ram's horn and gathered the army— offered David his own armor for the battle, even though Saul was larger than David. When David put on the king's armor he could barely walk, it was so big and bulky. David thanked the king but realized that he would have to fight on his own terms with his own weapons and not with anything that the king might give him.

So David went down to the stream and found five smooth stones that had been waiting in that stream for eons, being made smooth for just such an occasion. With his stones and a sling—that David had used to kill lions and bears that threatened his father's sheep—David walked onto the battlefield.

"The Lord is my shepherd . . ." David said as quietly as a prayer, speaking to himself. "I shall not want. Even though I walk through the valley of the shadow of death, I will fear no evil."

"What is this?" Goliath roared. "Why have you sent me a dog instead of a man, a boy instead of a warrior? Is this a joke?" Then Goliath turned to David and said, "Come closer, boy. I'll kill you quickly. You'll barely feel a thing."

No one is quite sure exactly what happened next. It is often that way with wars and battles. No one is ever quite sure how they start or the details of the battle because there is so much confusion. Whether the two armies faced off and began to fight while David ran up to Goliath, or whether David and Goliath stood on the plain facing one another while the armies looked on we cannot be sure. This much we do know: David put one smooth stone in his sling, hurled it at Goliath with all his might, hit the giant of a man between his eyes, and killed him. We know that the army of Israel chased down the Philistines that day and sent them running back to their own country. We know that Israel won a great victory that day—one they would never forget.

Sometimes when this story is told, it is told as just another war story, a story of who killed whom, who won and who lost. But every so often the story is told a different way. What is told is not so much the victory, but the way the victory was won. It is told as a story about the faith of the young man who went to a stream and pulled out five smooth stones—a young man who went into battle with no armor, just a heart full of faith in God, in his fellows, and in himself. When the story is told that way, it is more important than other war stories, because it gives us a hint of how we should live and how we should pray. It fills us with faith in the same God who inspired David thousands of years ago. Then it is a story that calls us even today to be faithful disciples.

COMMENTARY

The story of David and Goliath is a traditional Bible story for children, but it is seldom preached to adults. Often the storyteller emphasizes the difference in size between David, the boy, and Goliath, the giant. There are, however, other aspects of the story that will engage children: the relationship between brothers, the visual imagery of David in Saul's armor, the chaos of the battle scene.

It is a story that has elements of both the scandal and the claim of the gospel. The scandal is the violence, the idea that God might actually work out God's purposes through war and mayhem. The claim is David's faithfulness. God would have each of us possess such faith.

Chapter 3

Resources for the Liturgical Year

Advent

1

(This liturgy for lighting the candles on the Advent wreath may be used in a variety of settings.)

FIRST SUNDAY IN ADVENT

We light this first candle in the season of Advent because God sent Jesus to be the Messiah—the "anointed one." Jesus is that Messiah—the Christ—because God anointed him to be the Savior who would rescue us from sin and death. (FC 22)

Light one candle.

Prayer: Come to us this day, O God, come to us with light. Speak to us your truth and dwell with us in love. We give thanks, for in Christ every one of your promises is a "Yes." Through him, we are able to say "Amen," to the glory of God. **Amen.**

SECOND SUNDAY IN ADVENT

We light the second candle because Jesus Christ has come to us as the prophet of God. He was God's Word to a dying and sinful world; he embodied the love he proclaimed. Through Christ's birth, his life, death, and resurrection, Jesus became the great Yes that continues to be spoken by God, no matter how often we have said No. (SC 39)

Light the second Advent candle.

Prayer: God of the Prophets, give us this day the prophetic word of hope, that in moments of fear and despair we might look to you, our only source of comfort. Enable us to open our hearts, so that we might have Christ in us. **Amen.**

THIRD SUNDAY IN ADVENT

We light the third candle in honor of Jesus Christ, our great high priest. Jesus was the Lamb of God that took away the sin of the world. He became both our priest and sacrifice. Though we are a people sitting in deep darkness, although God looks upon our hopelessness in sin and death, Jesus Christ has rescued us, offering himself—his entire person and work—in order to reconcile us to God. (SC 40)

Light the third Advent candle.

Prayer: Dear God, our Good Shepherd, empower our lives to be filled with love, for we know that in loving others we bear witness to Christ's love for us. We long for a day when we will no longer be separated from God. **Amen.**

FOURTH SUNDAY IN ADVENT

We light the fourth candle in the name of Jesus Christ, our King. Jesus is the Lord who took the form of a servant. He perfected royal power in weakness. With no sword but the sword of righteousness, with no power but the power of love, Christ has defeated sin, evil, and death by reigning from the cross. (SC 41)

Light the fourth Advent candle.

Prayer: Dear God, with angels we would sing, "Glory to God in the highest, and on earth, peace." In Jesus Christ, we have seen the Prince of Peace, and we long for his return and the reign of peace, mercy, and good will. **Amen.**

2

(May be used on the First Sunday in Advent.)

Our Advent journey begins with a faithful God who chose the people of Israel to make a new beginning. They received God's covenant and prepared the way for Jesus to come as our Savior.

What is the covenant?

The covenant is an everlasting agreement between God and Israel.

What is in this agreement?

When God called Abraham and Sarah, God promised to bless their family, which was later called Israel. Through the people of Israel, God vowed to bless all the peoples of the earth. God promised to be Israel's God, and they promised to be God's people. God vowed to love Israel and to be their hope forever, and Israel vowed to worship and serve only God.

How did God keep this covenant?

God led Israel out of slavery in Egypt, gave them the Ten Commandments through Moses, and brought them into the land that God had promised.

Did the people keep their covenant with God?

Though some remained faithful, the people too often worshiped other gods and did not love each other as God commanded. They showed us how much we all disobey God's law.

What did God do to bring them back to the covenant?

Although God judged the people when they sinned, God still loved them and remained faithful to them. God sent them prophets to speak God's word. God gave them priests to make sacrifices for their sins. God called kings to protect the needy and guarantee justice. At last God promised to send the Messiah.

Then let us begin our Advent journey as we, too, wait and prepare for the coming of the Messiah. (FC 14–17, 20–21)

Christmas

1

LITANY, USING JOHN 1 AND STUDY CATECHISM
"In the beginning was the Word." (John 1:1a)

God is a God of love, a love that is powerful beyond measure. (SC 7)

"The Word was with God, and the Word was God." (1:1b)

The God who made heaven and earth has become God incarnate—God with us—in a wonderful and awe-inspiring way. (SC 35)

"In him was life, and the life was the light of all people." (1:4)

Our Lord Jesus Christ, crucified and risen, is himself God's promise that suffering will come to an end, that death shall be no more, and that all things will be made new. (SC 14)

"That light shines in the darkness and the darkness did not overcome it." (1:5)

Through Jesus Christ—his life of compassion, his death on the cross, and his resurrection from the dead—we see how vast is God's love for the world; a love ready to suffer for our sakes, yet so strong that nothing will prevail against it. (SC 8)

"The Word became flesh and lived among us, . . . full of grace and truth." (1:14)

By the Holy Spirit, we are made one with the Lord Jesus Christ. As members of this community of faith, we trust in God's Word, share in the Lord's Supper, and turn to God constantly in prayer. As we grow in grace and knowledge, we are led to do the good works that God intends for our lives. (SC 4)

2

OPENING PRAYER

Lord Jesus—Messiah, Redeemer, Christ: We greet your morning with joy. We give thanks for Christmas joy: for the generous spirit that inspires us to share gifts and renew friendships; for hearts warmed by the love of dear ones and the greeting of strangers. We thank you for the gift of your life. As God's anointed one, you are the perfect prophet, priest, and king. You are God's Word to a dying and sinful world, and you are the Lamb who takes away the sin of the world. You are the Lord who took the form of a servant and reigns with the sword of righteousness and the power of love. This place, our church, has become Bethlehem this happy morning. As this place has been transformed by your presence, we ask you to transform our joy into new life in you. **Amen**. (SC 38–41; FC 26).

Epiphany

1

CALL TO WORSHIP

Although we have no star to guide us,

we have gathered in this place in order to find and follow the Christ.

Although we have not been brought to our knees like the ancient Magi,

our desire to worship God is deep and powerful.

We do not bear gifts of gold, frankincense, and myrrh.

We offer food and shelter, justice and friendship, forgiveness and gospel.

God has made salvation available to all human beings through Jesus Christ, crucified and risen.

No one will be lost who can be saved.

God's story continues. Good news abounds. There is a living Christ to discover and worship and serve.

Let us rejoice and be glad. (SC 49, 51, 65).

2

PRAYER OF GREAT THANKSGIVING (INTRODUCTORY SECTION
ESPECIALLY FOR EPIPHANY)

> Celebrant: The Lord be with you.
>
> People: **And also with you.**
>
> Celebrant: Lift up your hearts.
>
> People: **We lift them to the Lord.**
>
> Celebrant: Let us give thanks to the Lord our God.
>
> People: **It is right to give our thanks and praise.**

We thank you, God, for sending a star to guide the wise ones to the Christ child. But even more, we praise you for signs and witnesses in every generation that lead us to your Christ. We thank you for the covenant made first with Israel—promising to be Israel's light and salvation. You made Israel your people and promised that through them all the peoples of the world would be blessed. (SC 36)

We thank you for prophets who declared your Word; for priests who made sacrifices for the sins of many; and for kings and rulers who ruled with justice, lifted up the poor and needy, and defended the people from their enemies. (SC 36)

With the apostles, prophets, and martyrs, with all those through the ages who have loved the Lord Jesus Christ, and with all who strive to serve him on earth here and now, we join our voices in offering praise to the God of loving power and powerful love. (SC 10)

Holy, holy, holy Lord, God of power and might,
Heaven and earth are full of your glory.
Hosanna in the highest.
Blessed is he who comes in the name of the Lord.
Hosanna in the highest.

With the coming of Jesus, the covenant with Israel was expanded and confirmed. Through Christ, the gates of salvation have been thrown open. Just as the Magi were welcomed at the cradle of the Christ child, so God welcomes all strangers and needy into the covenant of blessing. (SC 37) Jesus Christ offered food to the hungry and water to the thirsty; offered shelter to the wanderer, justice to the oppressed, friendship to the lonely, kinship to the faithful. Jesus forgave sins, preached good news, and filled all people with the hope of new life. (SC 65)

Jesus took upon himself the full consequences of our sinfulness—even the agony of abandonment by God—in order that we might be spared. But our Lord could not be held by the power of death. Jesus appeared to his followers, (Triumphant from the grave), in a new life. He has shown us his hands and feet in order that we might know that the one who was crucified is the Lord and Savior of the world. (SC 44, 46)
(Continue with memorial acclamation and conclusion of Great Prayer.)

The Baptism of the Lord

1

(May be used if baptisms are celebrated on the Sunday of the Baptism of the Lord.)

"In those days Jesus came from Nazareth of Galilee and was baptized by John in the Jordan. And just as he was coming up out of the water, he saw the heavens torn apart and the Spirit descending like a dove on him. And a voice came from heaven, 'You are my Son, the Beloved; with you I am well pleased.'" (Mark 1:9–11)

We, too, are children of God.

We belong to God, who loves us.
We are God's children by grace. (FC 1, 2, 3)

2

(When children are baptized who are not old enough to make their profession of faith, but who are beginning to understand that God loves them, the following questions may be asked of them after the questions to the parents presenting them for baptism.)

  Minister: Who are you?

  Child(ren): **I am a child of God.** (FC 1)

  Minister: What does it mean to be a child of God?

  Child(ren): **That I belong to God, who loves me.** (FC 2)

  Minister: When we baptize, we show that all of us are children of God and the Spirit seals us in God's love.

Transfiguration

PRAYER OF THE DAY

Living Christ, whose glory was revealed on earth, transfigured on a mountain, and tortured on a cross: Startle us with glory. Reveal to us a true vision of your glory so that we may know that you are the object of our worship, the self-revelation of God, and the Savior of the world. (SC 33) May our worship honor God as the source of all good things, until we are like mirrors reflecting the great beam of love that God shines on us. **Amen**. (SC 18)

Lent

PENITENTIAL LITANY FOR LENT

Merciful God, we confess that we have turned away from you and fallen into sin. We put ourselves in the center of our world; we think of ourselves first and others later.

We have turned away from you and fallen into sin. (FC 10)

We fail to pray and read our Bibles as we should;
we fail to give to others; we eat much while others have little.

We have turned away from you and fallen into sin.

Our relationship with you is broken
and our relations with others are confused.

We have turned away from you and fallen into sin.

We have closed our hearts to you
and disobeyed your law.

We have turned away from you and fallen into sin.

Gracious God, we thank you that although you hate our sin,
you never stop loving us.
During this Lenten season, help us to return to you,
receive forgiveness, and claim the new life offered by Jesus Christ.
Help us to reclaim our status as your beloved children. (FC 10–13)
Through Jesus Christ, who suffered, died, and rose for us, we pray. **Amen.**

Easter

1

OPENING SENTENCES
Why do Christians gather for worship on the first day of the week?

**Because it is the day when God raised our Lord Jesus from the dead.
Our hearts are glad with the memory of our Lord's resurrection.** (FC 39*)*

How do we know that Jesus is Lord?

**Jesus could not be held by the power of death.
Having died on the cross, he appeared to his followers, both men and
     women.
Showing them his hands and feet, the one who was crucified revealed
     himself as the Lord and Savior of the world.** (FC 28)

Christ is risen!

**Christ is risen indeed!
Alleluia!**

2

CHARGE AND BENEDICTION (IN THE FORM OF JOHN 21:15–19)
Children of God, do you love the One who created you?

We do love you, O God, and will worship you.

Children of God, do you love the One who created you?

We do love you, O God, and will love others.

Children of God, do you love the One who created you?

We do love you, O God, and will respect what you have created.

May God bless you and encourage you in all that you do. (FC 6)

Pentecost

CALL TO WORSHIP
The Spirit gathers us to worship God
and builds us up in faith, hope, and love,
so that we may go into the world to proclaim the gospel
and work for justice and peace. (FC 38)
Let us worship God together.

AFFIRMATION OF FAITH

1

We believe that the Holy Spirit was given to the first Christians
on the day of Pentecost. (FC 30)

That same Spirit filled the first Christians with joy
by revealing what Jesus has done for us.
We believe the Spirit inspired them to understand and proclaim the gospel,
and to live a new life together in thanksgiving to God. (FC 33)
The Holy Spirit also moves us to understand and believe the gospel,
gives us strength and wisdom to live by it,
and unites us into the community we call the church. (FC 34)

2

(See also Affirmation of Faith 4 based on the third article of the Apostles'
Creed on p. 20.)

CHARGE AND BENEDICTION
We are the church!

People who believe the good news about Jesus. (FC 35)

We are the church!

Gathered by the Holy Spirit, built up in faith, hope, and love. (FC 38)

We are the church!

**Sent out by God's Spirit to proclaim the gospel and to work for justice
and peace.**

Go in peace.

We go in the name of Jesus Christ. (FC 35, 38–39)

Chapter 4

Special Occasions

1

WELCOMING CHILDREN TO WORSHIP

(Question 40 describes the church at worship. When young children are "officially" welcomed to worship, this question can be incorporated into a brief ritual of welcome.)

Today we welcome our five (four, six) year olds to worship. Just as Jesus welcomed children and blessed them, so we welcome these children to our assembly. Let us remind ourselves what we do in Christian worship.

We adore and praise God.
We pray, sing hymns, and listen to readings from the Bible.
We also give offerings to God for the work of the church
and commit ourselves to serve God and our neighbors.
Above all, we hear the preaching of the gospel and celebrate the
**   sacraments.** (FC 40)

2

PRESENTATION OF BIBLES TO CHILDREN

(Questions 35–37 are adapted into a litany for the congregation to use on the day that Bibles are presented to children or youth. These questions and answers clarify for children and others why the Bible is such an important gift to the children.)

What is the church?

**We are the church: the people who believe the good news about Jesus,
who are baptized,
and who share in the Lord's Supper.
Through these means of grace,
the Spirit renews us so that we may serve God in love.**

How do we know this good news?

**Through reading the Bible and hearing it taught and preached.
The Holy Spirit inspired those who wrote the Bible
and helps us rely on its promises today.** (FC 35, 37)

Children's Prayer

**Dear God, as we read and study our Bibles,
by your Spirit help us to learn about your love for us in Jesus Christ.
Help us to learn how to follow you. Amen.**

Congregational Prayer

**Holy God, when these children were baptized,
we promised to guide and nurture them by word and deed,
with love and prayer, encouraging them to know and follow Christ
and to be faithful members of his church.
We pledge ourselves anew to this promise. Amen.**

3

PRESENTATION OF BIBLES TO YOUTH

(If the congregation makes a special presentation of study Bibles to youth,
two questions of the Study Catechism [56–57] may be incorporated into the
presentation liturgy.)

What do you mean when you speak of "the Word of God"?

**"Jesus Christ, as he is attested for us in Holy Scripture,
is the one Word of God which we have to hear
and which we have to trust and obey in life and in death"** (Barmen
    Declaration, Article I, BC 8.11). (SC 56)

Is not Holy Scripture also the Word of God?

**Yes, Holy Scripture is also God's Word because of its content,
its function, and its origin.
Its central content is Jesus Christ, the living Word.
Its basic function is to deepen our love, knowledge, and service
of him as Savior and Lord.
Its ultimate origin is in the Holy Spirit,
who spoke through the prophets and apostles, and who inspires us with
    eager desire for the truths that Scripture contains.** (SC 57)

Will you promise to be diligent and prayerful in your study of God's Word?

I will, with God's help.

4

(May be used for presentation of Bibles or catechisms to children or youth.)

We are God's covenant people.

What is the covenant?

The covenant is an everlasting agreement between God and Israel.

What is in this agreement?

**When God called Abraham and Sarah, God promised to bless their fam-
ily, which was later called Israel. Through the people of Israel, God
vowed to bless all the people of the earth and to be their God. (FC 15, 16)**

How are we to understand ourselves to be in this covenant?

Through the covenant with Abraham and Sarah and the new covenant in Jesus Christ, covenants of faith and grace, we are members of God's covenant family. Their story is our story, and the Bibles we present today tell that story—our story. (FC 23, 37)

5

CONFIRMATION OR REAFFIRMATION OF BAPTISMAL COVENANT (ESPECIALLY IF CELEBRATED ON THE DAY OF PENTECOST)

(May be incorporated into the liturgy for confirmation or reaffirmation of the baptismal covenant.)

The Holy Spirit was a gift to the church on the day of Pentecost.
How do you live in the communion of the Holy Spirit?

By the Holy Spirit, I am made one with the Lord Jesus Christ. I am baptized into Christ's body, the church. As a member of this community, I trust in God's Word, share in the Lord's Supper, and turn to God in prayer. As I grow in grace and knowledge, I am led to do the good works that God intends for my life. (SC: CV 4)

You have promised to be a faithful member of Christ's church. What is the church?

We are the church: the people who believe the good news about Jesus, who are baptized, and who share in the Lord's Supper.
Through these means of grace, the Spirit renews us so that we may serve God in love. (FC 35)

6

COMMISSIONING MISSION TRIP PARTICIPANTS

Today we commission these adults (*and youth*) who will show the mercy of Christ by working with people in (*location*). Friends, what is the mission of the church?

The mission of the church is to bear witness to God's love for the world in Jesus Christ. (SC 63)

What forms does this mission take?

The forms are as various as the forms of God's love, yet the center is always Jesus Christ. In the end it is always by Christ's mercy that the needs of the needy are met. (SC 64)

Who are the needy?

The hungry need bread, the homeless need a roof, the oppressed need justice, and the lonely need fellowship. At the same time—on another and deeper level—the hopeless need hope, sinners need forgiveness, the world needs the gospel. (SC 65)

Whom will you serve?

We serve our Lord Jesus Christ by (*brief description of mission work*).

Do you promise to show forth God's love as you serve in (*location*)?

I will, with God's help.

Question to Congregation

Will you promise to pray for these men and women as they go forth to show God's love and mercy in (*location*)?

We do.

Congregational Prayer

Gracious God, as we commission your servants, we pray that you will strengthen them for this work, build them up in love, and empower them to love others as you do. Amen.

7

TEACHER COMMISSIONING

"And Jesus came and said to them,
'All authority in heaven and on earth has been given to me.
Go therefore and make disciples of all nations,
baptizing them in the name of the Father and of the Son and of the Holy Spirit,
and teaching them to obey everything that I have commanded you.
And remember, I am with you always, to the end of the age'" (Matt. 28:18–20).
Jesus commissions his disciples
to make disciples, to baptize, and to teach.
You have been called to the ministry of teaching,
to which, today, we commission you.
The law of God is in that teaching.
What are the Ten Commandments?

The Ten Commandments are the law of God. When God gave them to Moses, God said, "I am the Lord your God, who brought you out of the land of Egypt, out of the house of slavery" (Exod. 20:2):

(1) You shall have no other gods before me.
(2) You shall not make for yourself an idol.
(3) You shall not make wrongful use of the name of the Lord your God.
(4) Remember the sabbath day, and keep it holy.
(5) Honor your father and your mother.
(6) You shall not murder.
(7) You shall not commit adultery.
(8) You shall not steal.
(9) You shall not bear false witness against your neighbor.
(10) You shall not covet what is your neighbor's.

What is the main point of these commandments?

You shall love the Lord your God with all your heart, mind, and strength; and you shall love your neighbor as yourself. (FC 18–19)

Friends, years from now your students may or may not be able to recite the Ten Commandments from memory, but they will remember that you loved the Lord your God with your whole heart, mind, and strength. They will remember that you loved your neighbor, yourself, and them. And they will remember that you taught them to do the same. In the words of our Lord Jesus Christ, "Go therefore and teach." **Amen.**

8

PRESENTATION OF BIBLES OR CATECHISMS

What are the Ten Commandments?

The Ten Commandments are the law of God.

When God gave them to Moses, God said, "I am the Lord your God who brought you out of the land of Egypt, out of the house of slavery."

God also said,

    (1) You shall have no other gods before me.
    (2) You shall not make for yourself an idol.
    (3) You shall not make wrongful use of the name of the Lord your God.
    (4) Remember the sabbath day, and keep it holy.
    (5) Honor your father and your mother.
    (6) You shall not murder.
    (7) You shall not commit adultery.
    (8) You shall not steal.
    (9) You shall not bear false witness against your neighbor.
  (10) You shall not covet what is your neighbor's.

What is the main point of these commandments?

You shall love the Lord your God with all your heart, mind, and strength; and you shall love your neighbor as yourself. (FC 18–19)

Today we present Bibles to our _____ . Just as the Ten Commandments are our guide for how we are to live with God and one another, so are the Scriptures our guide for faith and practice.

Chapter 5

Alternative Settings

1

CHRISTIAN EDUCATION WITH CHILDREN

Sunday evening or midweek series on the Lord's Prayer (FC 49–60 and SC 120–134), using the 10-chapter divisions in *Lord, Teach Us: The Lord's Prayer and the Christian Life,* by William H. Willimon and Stanley Hauerwas (Nashville: Abingdon Press, 1996, ISBN 0-687-00614-7). This resource is useful for adult study.

Enrichment activities could include singing, learning to sign the Lord's Prayer using American Sign Language (ASL), or involving participants in creating a movement translation of the prayer. Although there are suggested movements, it is especially effective if the participants, whether children, youth, or adults, create their own movements for each phrase.

2

PC (USA) Covenant People Curriculum Year 1, Unit 7, provides a five-session study of the Lord's Prayer for children from ages 3/4/5 through Grade 4. Available by calling 1-800-524-2612; ask for items #112072 and #11206 for ages 3/4/5; #113072 and #11306 for Grades 1–2; #114072 and #11406 for Grades 3–4. The second item number for each age/grade is a set of resource cards for art, drama, music, cooking, movement, storytelling, and even computer games that will enrich the curriculum to fill a traditional five-day Bible School for children. An evening intergenerational school could combine these materials and the suggestions for adult study listed above.

3

Another resource to assist in teaching with the catechism is the CD Rom "Rotating Workshops for Grades 1–5: Baptism, Communion, Apostles' Creed, Lord's Prayer." PC (USA), Congregational Ministries Publishing.

4

CHURCH SCHOOL ASSEMBLY

If elementary children gather before going to classrooms, provide copies of *Belonging to God: A First Catechism* and, depending on time, use one or more questions as a responsive reading with children serving as leaders. Choose questions that fit the liturgical season or themes the children will learn about in church school. Using the same set of questions for several weeks, such as using questions FC 22–24 throughout Advent, encourages and reinforces learning, and takes into account the irregular attendance of some children.

5

FAMILY WORSHIP

See "A Liturgy for Celebrating a Reaffirmation of Baptismal Covenant," pp. 32–33 and Lighting the Advent Candles, pp. 71–73. Suggestions for family worship can be found in *We Are the Family of God: Family Conversations about the Catechism.*

Resources for using the Lord's Prayer in family conversation and worship are located in *We Are the Family of God*, chapters 11 and 12, "A Family Conversation about the Lord's Prayer (I) and (II)"; *Get Ready! Get Set! Worship!* (Sharing Tree Publications, 2514 Swift, Houston, TX 77030. ISBN 0-9632053-0-7).

I Can Pray with Jesus is a helpful picture book for parents to share with children as they explore the meaning of the Lord's Prayer (See full reference on p. 97.)

Chapter 6

Book and Music Resources

CATECHISM RESOURCES

4 copies

Published by the Presbyterian Publishing Corporation

Book of Catechisms: Reference Edition (Geneva Press, 2001). Contains all three versions of the new catechisms with biblical references, as well as the Heidelberg Catechism and both of the Westminster Catechisms. ISBN 0-664-50153-2

STUDY CATECHISM RESOURCES
Published by the Presbyterian Publishing Corporation

The Study Catechism: Full Version (economy edition). Item #500692
The Study Catechism: Confirmation Version (economy edition). Item #500706
Can We Talk? Conversations for Faith (for confirmation and more). Teacher's Guide, Item #500927; Student Journal, Item #500935
Foundations of Faith: Education for New Church Members (based on the Apostles' Creed). Teacher's Guide, Item #500943; Student Guide, Item #500951
Devotion and Discipline: Training for Presbyterian Leaders (based on the Ten Commandments and the Lord's Prayer). Resource, Item #50096X

FIRST CATECHISM RESOURCES
Belonging to God: A First Catechism (children's edition, illustrated). Item #500560
Belonging to God: A First Catechism (gift edition). Item #500579

Belonging to God: A First Catechism (economy edition). Item #500684
Catechism Art Cards (60), Item #500595
Catechism Question Cards (60), Item #500587
✓*Children and Sacraments,* by Debbie Hough and Carol Wehrheim. Leader's
   Guide, Item #500617
✗*The Big Picture: A Resource for Confirmation and Preconfirmation,* by Korey
   E. Lowry and Kerri Peterson-Davis. Supplement for Leaders, Item
   #500633; Magazine resource, Item #500625
✓*Teaching the Catechism in Special Settings,* by Donald L. Griggs. Leader's
   Guide, Item #500609
✓*We Are the Family of God: Family Conversations about the Catechism,* by
   Ann Reed Held and Sally Stockley Johnson, Item #500641
Belonging to God Audiocassette or CD. Cassette Item #50065X; CD Item
   #500668

RESOURCES FOR TEACHING EITHER CATECHISM

Teaching the New Catechisms in Your Church (video), Item #B55502
Pastor's and Educator's Guide, Item #500676

ANNOTATED BOOK LIST

I. Identity and Creation: Questions 1–9

Baylor, Bird. *I'm in Charge of Celebrations.* 0-684-18579-2
A desert dweller celebrates wonders of the wilderness.

Brown, Judith Gwyn. *Bless All Creatures Here Below.* 0-8192-1665-8
A celebration for the blessing of animals.

Brown, Margaret Wise. *The Runaway Bunny.* 0-06-443018-9
A lovingly steadfast mother finds her child every time he runs away.

Castle, Caroline. *For Every Child.* 0-8037-2650-3
The U.N. rights of the child in words and pictures.

Grimes, Nikki. *At Break of Day.* 0-8028-5104-5
Jesus is present with God at the creation of the world.

Jeffs, Stephanie. *In the Beginning.* 0-687-08730-9
Retelling of the creation story for children ages 6–10.

Kasua, Masahiro. *The Beginning of the World.* 0-687-02765-9
Retelling of the creation story for young children.

Wood, Douglas. *Old Turtle.* 0-938586-48-3
A fable promoting deeper understanding of the earth and our relationship with it.

II. Sin: Questions 10–13

Bunting, Eve. *Terrible Things.* 0-8276-0325-8
An allegory of the Holocaust.

Hamilton, Virginia. *Sweet Whispers, Brother Rush.* 0-380651-93-9
A long-dead uncle helps Tree learn the necessity of forgiveness and the burden of sin.

Henkes, Kevin. *Lilly's Purple Plastic Purse.* 0-688-12897-1
Lilly does something to her favorite teacher for which she is very, very sorry.

Le Guin, Ursula. *A Wizard of Earthsea.* 0-553-26250-5
A young boy misuses his talent and unleashes a mysterious evil.

Seattle, Chief. *Brother Eagle, Sister Sky.* 0-8037-0969-2
Chief Seattle describes his people's love and respect for the earth and his concern for its destruction.

Zolotow, Charlotte. *The Quarreling Book.* 0-064430-34-0
The consequences of actions spiral downward until a forgiving dog turns things around.

III. Covenant and the Ten Commandments: Questions 14–21

Appelt, Kathi. *I See the Moon.* 0-8028-5118-5
The moon becomes a sign of God's love as a little child goes to sleep.

Le Tord, Bijou. *Sing a New Song: A Book of Psalms.* 0-8028-5139-8
Selected psalms in simple, praise-filled words accompanied by delicate watercolors (ages 4–6).

Paterson, John and Katherine. *Images of God.* 0-395-70734-X
Explores images the Bible uses to teach about God.

Thomas, Mack. *The Nursery Bible.* 0-88070-665-1
People in the Bible who heard God's voice (ages 2 and under).

IV. Jesus: Questions 22–29

The Nativity:

Davies, Taffy. *The New Star.* 0-687-08750-3
The nativity and life of Jesus with stunning space illustrations.

Paterson, Katherine. *Angels and Other Strangers: Family Christmas Stories.*
0-06-440283-5

————. *A Midnight Clear: Stories for the Christmas Season.* 0-525-67529-9

Vivas, Julie, illus. *The Nativity.* 0-15-200535-8
King James text accompanies whimsical illustrations.

Wojciechowski, Susan. *The Christmas Miracle of Jonathan Toomey.* 1-
56402-320-6
*A lonely woodcarver learns to open his heart to love as he carves special
nativity figures.*

Life of Jesus:

Chamberlain, Eugene. *Jesus, God's Son, Savior, Lord.* 0-8054-4226-X
Explores Jesus' life and meaning (currently out of print).

Gibbons, Gail. *Easter.* 0-8234-0737-3
Examines the background, significance, symbols, and traditions of Easter.

Lindvall, Ella K. *Read-Aloud Bible Stories*, Vols. 3 & 4. 0-8024-7165-X and
0-8024-7166-8
Selected stories for children ages 3–7.

Oursler, Fulton. *A Child's Life of Jesus.* 0-687-02910-4
Jesus' life and teachings adapted for children ages 5–10.

Wildsmith, Brian. *The Easter Story.* 0-8028-5189-4
Celebration of Holy Week and Easter through glorious illustrations.

————. *Jesus*. 0-8028-5212-2
Selected stories from Jesus' life with luminous illustrations.

V. Pentecost and the Holy Spirit: Questions 30–38

Fogle, Jeanne S. *Seasons of God's Love: The Church Year.* 0-664-25032-7
Explains the cycle of the liturgical year.

Fox, Mem. *Whoever You Are.* 0-15-200787-3
Despite differences, there are similarities that join people around the world.

Hamanaka, Sheila. *All the Colors of the Earth.* 0-688-11131-9
Celebrates that children of "all nations," all colors, are essentially the same.

Leimert, Karen Mezek. *All the Children of the World.* 0-8499-1310-1
Celebrates different cultures around the world, Iowa to Portugal.

Sasso, Sandy E. *In God's Name.* 1-879045-26-5
A spiritual celebration of all people of the world and their belief in one God.

VI. Worship and Sacraments: Questions 39–45

Boling, Ruth L. *A Children's Guide to Worship.* 0-664-50015-3
Helps children become familiar with the order of worship.

————. *Come Worship with Me.* 0-664-50045-5
A journey through the church year.

Cone, Milly. *The Story of Shabbat.* 0-06-027944-3
Explains the history and traditions of the Jewish Sabbath celebration.

Fogle, Jeanne S. *Signs of God's Love: Baptism and Communion.* 0-664-24636-2
Explains the sacraments using experiences familiar to children.

Grimes, Nikki. *Come Sunday.* 0-8028-5134-7
A little girl tells of a typical Sunday, from waking through the elements of worship.

Ramshaw, Gail. *1·2·3 Church*. 0-8066-2335-7
Illustrations and rhyming text featuring numbers present essentials of the Christian faith.

————. *Every Day and Sunday, Too*. 0-8066-2334-9
Links worship liturgy to everyday activities.

Sasso, Sandy Eisenberg. *In God's Name*. 1-879045-26-5
A spiritual celebration of all people of the world and their belief in one God.

Wangerin, Walter, Jr. *Water, Come Down! The Day You Were Baptized*. 0-8066-3711-0
The whole of creation joins family and friends in celebrating the baptism of a child.

VII. Prayer: Questions 46–60

Baynes, Pauline, illus. *Thanks Be to God*. 0-02-708541-4
Selected prayers from around the world.

Cooper, Floyd. *Cumbayah*. 0-688-13543-9
Multicultural illustrations accompany the text of the popular folk song.

Denham, Joyce. *A Child's Book of Celtic Prayers*. 0-8294-1077-5
Translations from Irish Gaelic poetry into English prose and verse.

Hague, Michael, illus. *A Child's Book of Prayers*. 0-8050-0211-1
Illustrated collection of short prayers and devotions.

Ladwig, Tim, illus. *The Lord's Prayer*. 0-8028-5180-0
Accompanying the text of the prayer are illustrations of a little girl and her father helping a neighbor.

Lindbergh, Reeve. *The Circle of Days*. 0-7637-0357-0
From St. Francis' Canticle of the Sun, rhyming text gives thanks for all creation.

————. *In Every Tiny Grain of Sand*. 0-7636-0176-4
Collection of prayers and praise from many traditions.

O'Neal, Debbie. *I Can Pray with Jesus: The Lord's Prayer for Children*. 0-8066-3328-X
Prayer text accompanied by simple explanations of each phrase.

Parry, Alan and Linda. *Little Prayer Series*:

Classic Children's Prayers
0-8499-1160-5
Mealtime Prayers   0-8499-1149-4
Prayers of Praise   0-8499-1159-1
Bedtime Prayers   0-8499-1148-6

Board books offering appropriate prayers for very young children.

Wilson, Anne, illus. *The Lord's Prayer*. 0-570-07132-1
Vibrant contemporary illustrations symbolizing each aspect of the prayer match the text.

Wood, Douglas. *Grandad's Prayers of the Earth*. 0-7636-0660-X
A boy finds comfort remembering his Grandad's teaching that all things in nature pray.

Congregational Song

There are many different sources for congregational music that represent different musical styles. The following is a listing of several sources and a few suggestions of specific music from those sources. Abbreviations are identified below.

Identity and creation (FC 1–9)

HH	#24	Um Menino (A Child)
HH	#11	El Cielo Canta (Heaven Is Singing)
HH	#15	Psalm 136 (Give Thanks Unto the Lord)
MFT1	p. 100	Jubilate Deo
PH	#294	Wherever I May Wander
TIOAU	p. 15	Be Still and Know

Sin (FC 10–13)

PH	#223	O My Soul, Bless Your Redeemer
PH	#403	What a Friend We Have in Jesus

SOZ   #95   I Want Jesus to Walk with Me
WP   #86   Kyrie Eleison

Covenant (FC 14–21)
HH   #14   O Give Thanks to the Lord
TIOAU   p. 44   Lo, I Am with You

Jesus as human (FC 24–26)
GATHER   #392   Lord, Who Throughout These Forty Days
GATHER   #393   Jesus Walked This Lonesome Valley
PH   #85   What Wondrous Love Is This
SOZ   #87   Calvary

Jesus as Savior and Lord (FC 22–23, 27–29)
CAYP   p. 94   Agnus Dei (St. Bride Setting)
HH   #30   Mantos y Palmas (Cloaks and Branches)
LUYH   p. 120   Lamb of God
LUYH   p. 81   Surely It Is God
WP   #19   Christ's Is the World in Which We Move
WP   #24   O Lamb of God, *Cordero Ng Dios*
WP   #64   O Lamb of God, *Hwayana YA-mwari*
WP   #78   Jesus the Lord Said
CAYP   p. 84   Behold, I Make All Things New

Holy Spirit/Pentecost (FC 30–38)
LUYH   p. 133   Come, Holy Spirit
LUYH   p. 85   Thy Word
MFT1   p. 36   Veni Sancte Spiritus
PH   #323   Loving Spirit
PH   #314   Like the Murmur of the Dove's Song

Worship and Sacraments (FC 39–45)
HH   #34   Come, Let Us Eat
LUYH   p. 127   Eat This Bread and Never Hunger
LUYH   p. 24   God Is So Good
LUYH   p. 47   Santo, Santo
MFT2   p. 30   Eat This Bread
PH   #507   I Come with Joy
PH   #508   For the Bread Which You Have Broken
PH   #513   Let Us Break Bread Together
PH   #514   Let Us Talents and Tongues Employ
WP   #50   Hallelujah, Hallelujah, You Are God
WP   #49   Alleluia! We Sing Your Praises

Baptism (FC 42–44)

GATHER	#809	There Is One Lord
LBW	#193	Cradling Children in His Arm
LBW	#195	This Is the Spirit's Entry Now
NCH	#323	Little Children Welcome
NHLC	#3	What King Would Wade Through Murky Streams
TH	#295	Sing Praise to Our Creator
UMH	#604	Praise and Thanksgiving Be to God
UMH	#605	Wash, O God, Our Sons and Daughters
UMH	#608	This Is the Spirit's Entry Now
UMH	#609	You Have Put On Christ
		Lord Jesus, Born a Tiny Child (Composed by Malcolm Archer for the 1999 Montreat Conferences on Worship and Music)

Prayer (FC 46–60)

CAYP	p. 71	Listen, Lord
LUYH	p. 109	Make Me a Channel of Your Peace
LUYH	p. 111	O Lord, Hear My Prayer
LUYH	p. 112	The Lord's Prayer
LUYH	p. 115	Everything Is Yours, Lord
LUYH	p. 65	Kind and Merciful God
MFT2	p. 46	O Lord, Hear My Prayer
WP	#107	My Prayers Rise

Sources

CAYP	*Come All You People,* John Bell and the Wild Goose Worship Group (GIA, 1994)
GATHER	*Gather* (GIA, 1994)
HH	*Halle, Halle: We Sing the World Round*, C. Michael Hawn (Choristers Guild, 1999)
LBW	*Lutheran Book of Worship* (Minneapolis: Augsburg Publishing House, 1978)
LUYH	*Lift Up Your Hearts* (Geneva Press, 1999)
MFT1	*Music from Taize*, Berthier (GIA)
MFT2	*Music from Taize, Volume 2,* Berthier (GIA)
NCH	*New Century Hymnal* (Pilgrim Press, 1995)
NHLC	*New Hymns for the Life of the Church*, Carol Doran and Thomas Troeger (Oxford University Press, 1992)
PH	*Presbyterian Hymnal* (Westminster John Knox Press, 1990)
SOZ	*Songs of Zion* (Abingdon Press, 1981)
TH	*The Hymnal, 1982* (Episcopal) (The Church Hymnal Corporation)
TIOAU	*There Is One Among Us*, John Bell and the Wild Goose Worship Group (GIA, 1999)

UMH   *United Methodist Hymnal* (1989)
WP   *World Praise*, ed. David Peacock and Geoff Weaver (Marshall Pick-
            ering/Harper Collins, 1995)

Anthems (Unison and SA)

The following is a sampling of anthems suitable for use with children's choirs.

Identity and Creation
Carol of Creation, Shirley McRae, Choristers Guild, CGA611
Child of God, Appalachian Carol, arr. Betty Ann Ramseth, Give Praises with Joy,
    Broadman, 1979
Clap Your Hands, Stamp Your Feet, Ronald A. Nelson, Leslie Brandt, Augsburg,
    11-0649
Do You Know Who Made the Day? Hal Hopson, Elizabeth Shields, Choristers
    Guild, CGA331
God Is Love, Betty Ann Ramseth, Trilby Jordan, Choristers Guild, CGA568
God Loves Me, Ruth White, Schmitt, Hall, & McCreary, SCH CH 244
God Made Me! Michael Jothen, Beckenhorst, BP1016
God's Great Lights, Helen Kemp, Concordia, 98-3072
In Heavenly Love, John Ness Beck, Beckenhorst, BP1404
I Will Love the Lord, Bedford, Choristers Guild, CGA419
Little Lamb, Who Made Thee? Hal Hopson, William Blake, Choristers Guild,
    CGA451
Miracle of Grace, Betty Ann Ramseth, Herbert Brokering, Choristers Guild,
    CGA241
Over All (Sobre Todos), Michael Jothen, Choristers Guild, CGA835

Sin
Create in Me a Clean Heart, Jeff Reeves, Choristers Guild, CGA879
Create in Me, O God, Jane Marshall, Choristers Guild, CGA750
Somebody's Knocking, James E. Clemens, Choristers Guild, CGA865
Somebody's Knockin' at Your Door, Spiritual, arr. Linda Spevacek, Lorenz
    10/1445K

Covenant
Dance and Sing, for the Lord Will Be with Us, Hebrew Folk Tune, arr. Hal Hop-
    son, Choristers Guild, CGA749
Sing, Dance, Clap Your Hands, Hebrew Folk Tune, arr. Ziegenhals, Choristers
    Guild CGA625

Thanks Be to Thee, G. F. Handel, H.W. Gray, CMR1422

Jesus as Human
Jesus' Hands Were Kind Hands, French Folk Tune, arr. Sue Ellen Page, Margaret Cropper, Choristers Guild, CGA485
Lenten Love Song, Helen Kemp, Choristers Guild, CGA486
The Lost Sheep, John Horman, Choristers Guild, CGA308

Jesus as Savior and Lord
God So Loved the World, John Horman, Choristers Guild, CGA447
I Am the Light, Ralph Johnson, Augsburg, 11-1679
I Am the Vine, Allen Pote, Sacred Music Press, S-8636
I'm the Good Shepherd, Daniel Barta, Choristers Guild, CGA861
Lenten Prayer, Robert J. Powell, Billie Echols, Choristers Guild, CGA159
You Are the Branches, Michael Jothen, Choristers Guild, CGA755

Holy Spirit/Pentecost
Like the Murmur of the Dove's Song, David Ashley White, Carl Daw, Choristers Guild, CGA352
Like the Murmur of the Dove's Song, Peter Cutts, arr. Michael A. Burkhardt, Carl Daw, Morning Star MSM-60-5000
Loving Spirit, Helen Kemp, Shirley Erena Murray, Choristers Guild, CGA862
Offertory for Pentecost 7, Robert Hobby, Morning Star, MSM-80-575

Worship and Sacraments
Taste and See (Psalm 34), Randolph Currie, GIA, G-2824

Baptism
See This Wonder in the Making, Carl Schalk, Jaroslav Vajda, Morning Star, MSM-50-8400
You Have Put on Christ, Howard Hughes, GIA, G-2283

Prayer
For Hard Things, Jane Marshall, Edith Kent Battle, Choristers Guild, CGA618
Prayer for Today, Margaret Tucker, Mary M. Coulson, Choristers Guild, CGA358
Prayer of St. Francis, Helen Litz, St. Francis of Assisi, Choristers Guild, CGA242
Your Trusting Child, Shirley McRae, Choristers Guild, CGA614

Commissioned Hymn Text

"I AM A CHILD OF GOD"

Based on *Belonging to God: A First Catechism,* especially questions 1–9.

1

I am a child of God,
The One who made and keeps me.
By God's free gift of love
God's child I always will be.
Forever I belong.
I know that this is true,
And with my mind and heart
I trust and love God too.

2

God's image is in us,
The people of creation.
No matter where we live,
We share a close relation.
God's covenant is sure,
Eternal word for all
Who follow in God's way
And answer to God's call.

3

God never turns from us,
Not even in our sinning.
God loves and waits for us
To claim a new beginning.
By opening our hearts
We then prepare the way
For God's love to come in
And guide us every day.

4

I thank God for that love
And all the world around me,
The seen and unseen things,
And promised things that will be.
Through worship, trust, and prayer
May I reflect God's will.
Let love be seen in me
As I God's word fulfill.

Mary Jackson Cathey
Suggested tune: NUN DANKET ALLE GOTT 6.7.6.7.6.6.6.6.

THE LORD'S PRAYER

There are two musical settings of the Lord's Prayer included in this resource because of the primacy of the Lord's Prayer in the liturgical, musical, and devotional life of God's people. The first is a new setting composed by John Horman, commissioned for this resource, and it incorporates the ecumenical version that is found in the catechisms. The anthem was composed for children's choirs, but it can be used by other choral ensembles and the congregation.

The other is an older setting, long out of print, which still has musical merit. This setting of the Lord's Prayer was first published in Presbyterian Sunday school curriculum for young children in the late 1940s. It is lovely and singable and offers a memorable way to teach the prayer to children five and older or to enhance a congregation's prayer experience through unison singing. It could be sung as a children's choir anthem as well.

The recently published service music resource *Holy Is the Lord* (Geneva Press, 2002) contains other musical settings of the Lord's Prayer as does the *Presbyterian Hymnal.*

The Lord's Prayer

Based on Mathew 6:9–14

John D. Horman

The Lord's Prayer

(Unison Song)

Albert Johnson

Our Fa - ther,_____ who art in heav - en, Hal - low - ed be Thy

name. Thy king - dom come. Thy will be done on earth as it

is in heav - en. Give us this day our dai - ly bread. And for - give us our debts, as

we for-give our debt-ors.___ And lead us not in-to temp-ta-tion, but de - liv-er us from e - vil: For

Thine is the king-dom, and the power, and the glo-ry, for ev - - - er. A - men.